This book belongs to

_____

A woman who
finds rest in
God alone
(Psalm 62:1)

When Women Long for Rest

CINDI McMENAMIN

HARVEST HOUSE PUBLISHERS

EUGENE, OREGON

Cover by Koechel Peterson & Associates, Inc., Minneapolis, Minnesota

Cover photo © Antony Nagelmann/Taxi/Getty Images

Some of the names have been changed to protect the anonymity and privacy of the women who shared their stories in this book.

WHEN WOMEN LONG FOR REST

Copyright © 2004 by Cindi McMenamin
Published by Harvest House Publishers
Eugene, Oregon 97402

Library of Congress Cataloging-in-Publication Data

McMenamin, Cindi, 1965–
  When women long for rest / Cindi McMenamin.
  p. cm.
  Includes bibliographical references.
  ISBN 0-7369-1130-8 (pbk.)
  1. Christian women—Religious life. 2. Rest—Religious aspects—Christianity. I. Title.
  BV4527.M4329 2004
  248.8'43—dc22   2003023491

Printed in the United States of America

04   05   06   07   08   09   10   11   / VP-CF /   10   9   8   7   6   5

As David once said, "My soul finds rest in God alone" (Psalm 62:1).

This one's for You, Lord. Thank You for the lesson.

Acknowledgments

Thank you to some friends who, perhaps unknowingly, helped make this book happen:

- My friend, Edie Davis—for your wise words over lunch one day.
- My friend and partner in ministry, Chris Castillero—for encouraging me to rest, and for standing by me...always.
- My friend and "brother," Paul Lopez—for walking me through the storm and helping me learn more about humility, rest, and trust than I ever thought I wanted to learn.
- My editor and friend, Steve Miller, at Harvest House Publishers, for encouraging me to write when the convictions came.
- My husband and best friend, Hugh, for recognizing our need for rest and making sure it happens regularly.
- My daughter and best girlfriend, Dana, for reminding me to slow down and "seize the day."

And above all, I'm grateful to the Lord Jesus Christ, the "stiller of storms" and the Giver of rest.

Contents

It's Time to Get Away

Why are we so tired and stressed these days? Ask any woman and you'll probably hear many of the same responses:

"There's so much to *do*...I just can't seem to get it all done."

"I've overcommitted myself...again."

"I'm overwhelmed by my responsibilities."

"There are too many demands on my time."

Somehow, somewhere, we've gotten the idea that we must do it *all*. Along the way, we've lost our joy...and sometimes even the ability to do *anything* at all.

Look at the cover of any woman's magazine and you'll find the word *stress* dominates the headlines: "Lose the Stress!" "10 Habits of Stressless Women," "79 Beat-Stress Ideas," "Renew, Recharge, Relax." The promises of rest and relief abound. But believe me, they don't work. I've tried them. And so have countless other women who are still feeling weary and overwhelmed.

On a recent speaking trip, I was sitting at an outdoor café with some women from the church where I was to speak that evening. Even though we were in the grasslands of Twin Falls, Idaho, where we weren't interrupted by the sounds of cell phones or barraged by endless traffic noise, these women were longing for rest. Sue was retired and said she's busier now than when she was working full-time. Mary was married, with no children, but still tired from the rush and pace of her career life. Trisha was married, with a two-year-old boy and a six-month-old baby, and found little time to eat her lunch, let alone fulfill her other responsibilities. And Karen was middle-aged and single, and struggling with high blood pressure and the inability to say no. Although all these women were in different seasons of life and lived in different circumstances, they all had one thing in common: They were exhausted. Exhausted from work. Worn out from responsibilities at home and church. Tired from juggling children's or grandchildren's activities. Overwhelmed by their pace of life.

Why *is* it that we are so tired these days?

Some say it's because technology has invaded every corner of our lives, as evidenced by our cell phones going off all day, emails that scream to be answered immediately, instant messages that pop up on us at any given time, and that constant pressure to keep burning the midnight oil because time is running short. Others say it's because we live in a world that's wired for sound, and we can't seem to shut out the noise. Still others believe we bring exhaustion upon ourselves by trying to do everything— taking advantage of every opportunity that comes our way, trying to get our children in every sport and extracurricular activity, and trying to fulfill nearly every obligation that's placed upon us. I say it's a little of everything. But mostly, it's that we don't know how to rest anymore. We are constantly striving, obsessed with productivity, driven by perfectionism, consumed by competition, and exhausted from endless activity.

I was there, too, thinking there was no alternative to a stressful but productive life. "If I'm busy, it must mean I'm successful" was the motto I hid behind. Until I couldn't hide any longer. In the midst of the flurry of busyness, a still small voice whispered, "Come away with Me…this is not how I intended for you to live."

When I listened to that voice and learned what it meant to get away with Him—away from the busyness of the world, away from the pressures of others, away from a myriad of expectations I had placed on myself—I found true peace. And purpose. And a pace that no longer overwhelmed me.

In this book I will tell you the story of how God revealed to me a slower and more satisfying path toward a life of fulfillment *and* rest, but for now just let me tell you that after seeing the dramatic difference between a rushed life and a rested one—and experiencing the peace that a balanced, sane life can bring—I can never go back to a life in which I allowed relentless pressure to steal my joy. And why would I ever want to?

I imagine *you* are feeling weary and overwhelmed with life as well. Can you relate to one of the psalmists, who said: "Oh, how I wish I had wings like a dove; then I would fly away and rest! I would fly far away to the quiet of the wilderness"? (Psalm 55:5-7 NLT). In another translation those words sound more like a desperate plea than a distant wish for relief: "Get me out of here on dove wings; I want some peace and quiet. I want a walk in the country, I want a cabin in the woods. I'm *desperate* for a change from rage and stormy weather" (THE MESSAGE).

If you, too, are desperate for a change, then you're in the right place…the place where you can experience God's peace for your overwhelmed life and the real rest you've been longing for.

Several months ago I was desperate for a change as well. I'd been thinking long and hard about where I would end up in another five years if I continued at a burnout pace. Did I want to become exhausted and worn out, unhealthy because of the toll that stress was placing on my life? Or did I want to grow more peaceful and serene through the years, constantly revived and refreshed by living lightly and freely? I realized that I wanted my life to reflect a growing *beauty* from my relationship with the Lord, not a growing busyness. I wanted the result of my walk with God to be *refreshment*, not weariness. I wanted to revel in the relationship, not live in the hurriedness. I realized then the way things should be: The more I know Him and the more I grow with Him, the more beautiful my heart and life should become. But it seemed just the opposite had happened with me: The more I wanted to please Him, the more I *did* for Him, the more *busy* my life had become.

We all know of women who have grown more haggard through the years because of the stress in their lives. How could I, instead, become a woman who grows closer to God and more relaxed, more serene, more mature with each passing year? This wasn't a question about external beauty and how to avoid the aging process. It was a question about inner beauty and deep soul work. This was a matter of rest...*real* rest. The more I sit at God's feet, the more I will be at rest with Him and the more my heart will sing, my spirit will soar, and my eyes will shine. *That's* the kind of woman I want to be...a woman who kisses goodbye the wrinkles of worry and develops a life that rests in the Almighty and radiates with the beauty of a woman who is rested, rejuvenated, and refreshing to all around her.

But how is that possible?

At the most demanding times in Jesus' life—when crowds of people were pressing in on Him to be taught, to be healed, to be near Him—He did what I believe He's calling us to do in the midst of a hectic life today. He withdrew to rest.

"Come with me by yourselves to a quiet place and get some rest," He told his friends in Mark 6:31. Doesn't that sound inviting? To get away with Jesus to a quiet place and get some rest? You'll be delighted to know His invitation still stands.

Jesus' desire to withdraw and be strengthened by rest and quiet is a powerful example to us today of what to do in the midst of all our busyness, even if we feel we're too important to "step away" from it all. Jesus Himself said in Matthew 11:28-30, "Come to me, all of you who are weary and carry heavy burdens, and I will give you rest. Take my yoke upon you. Let me teach you, because I am humble and gentle, and you will find rest for your souls. For my yoke fits perfectly, and the burden I give you is light" (NLT).

When I read that passage in *The Message*, the beauty of that invitation from Jesus took my breath away:

> Are you tired? Worn out? Burned out on religion? Come to me. Get away with me and you'll recover your life. I'll show you how to take a real rest. Walk with me and work with me—watch how I do it. Learn the unforced rhythms of grace. I won't lay anything heavy or ill-fitting on you. Keep company with me and you'll learn to live freely and lightly.

Oh, to live freely and lightly! To know what it means to take a "real rest." To know by heart the "unforced rhythms of grace" Jesus modeled when He walked (rather than ran) on this earth.

Something has to change, my friend, doesn't it?

Are *you* ready to take Jesus up on His invitation to live freely and lightly? Then come with me on this journey as we learn to rest in this world that is constantly running. Come with me as we strip away from our life the externals of busyness *for* God and go deeper in a relationship *with* Him. Come with me and recover the *rest* of your life! I promise you, once you discover it, you'll never want to go back. It's all about learning how to get away with Him—every day—in your heart. This book will show you how.

*J*esus, in the unbroken intimacy of His Father's love, kept a quiet heart. None of us possesses a heart so perfectly at rest, for none lives in such divine unity, but we can learn a little more each day of what Jesus knew....

ELISABETH ELLIOT

ONE

Following God's Call to Be Still

WHY DO WE FEEL SO GUILTY WHEN WE'RE NOT doing anything? I know, if you sleep in a few extra hours, blow off an afternoon by reading a book, or find yourself just sitting and staring into space, you hear that familiar voice ring through your head: "*Do something! You're wasting time.*"

Where did we get this idea that we must constantly be doing something?

In our flurry of activity, our juggling of roles and responsibilities, and our scampering around because of the time pressures on our lives, a still small voice whispers to us: *Come away with Me to a quiet place where we can get some rest.*

Jesus spoke that to His disciples after a long, weary day in ministry (Mark 6:31). Yes, even the Son of God grew weary and knew when He needed to rest. Today, the Son of God knows when *we're* weary and need to rest.

I find it refreshing to read in Genesis 2:2 that after God created the heavens and the earth, He rested. Even *God* rested. So, if God Almighty took time to rest, shouldn't we?

Now, it wasn't because God was tired. God didn't physically need the rest, as our bodies do. But He was modeling something to the man and woman made in His image. He was modeling to us a "coming away" from labor to revel in the enjoyment of life. He didn't want us to be so consumed by our work that we neglected worship. He didn't want us so busy "making and producing" that we couldn't spend time enjoying what *He* made for us. He was showing us what our lives should look like—a balance of rest and work.

When God created a Sabbath day, He was literally setting aside time for us to pause, as the word *Sabbath* literally means to "cease" or "desist." "The idea is not that of relaxation or refreshment, but cessation from activity."[1] Which particular day this rest is observed wasn't the point. What, in particular, could or could not be done on that day wasn't the point either. The point was that God wanted us to regularly practice that "ceasing" or "coming away" with Him to rest, revel in our relationship with Him, and enjoy all He has made and given us.

God Woos Us to Rest

In His Word, God woos us to rest, to be still and know He is God (Psalm 46:10), to come to Him and lay down our burdens so we can experience rest (Matthew 11:28). He woos us to rest as a way of coming back to Him and remembering who He is and what He has done for us (in all that He's created, all He's given us, all He is). Yet in the Bible, we're often told His people "would not listen."[2]

There was a time when I wouldn't listen, either.

It had been a whirlwind month for me. I'd been speaking every weekend and was trying to keep a house, tend to my pastor-husband's needs, raise a daughter, serve on several boards and organizations, and run a church women's ministry at the same time. And I was exhausted. I had gone away to a weekend retreat with my church's women, but I could stay only one day, as I would have to catch a 5:00 A.M. flight the next morning for a three-city media tour to promote my newest book.

I never took the time at the retreat to really rest, but apparently God was not going to have that! As I sat down on a Saturday morning, just hours before I'd leave to go home and pack up again for my next trip, I read this from Isaiah 28:12: "This is the resting place, let the weary rest." Something pulled at my heart at that moment.

Where is the resting place? Here? At this retreat center in the mountains? Where, God? Because I have to leave in a little while, anyway! But His words continued to penetrate my heart: *This is the resting place. Let the weary rest.*

Suddenly, I got it. This was where it stopped. This was the point in time at which I was to slow down and live sanely again. This was where God intervened and said, "Enough!" Something in my life needed to change so I could come back to the depth of the relationship that I had once shared with my God. And God knew that. Something happened in my heart that day as I realized I wasn't the only one who felt I was tired and needed rest. God longed for me to come back to the relationship with Him where I rested in Him and wasn't trying to do everything myself. He missed the intimacy, too. He was tired of me being too tired for Him. He desired for me to rest and rejuvenate and reunite with Him, too.

My heart was convicted as I realized my running to and fro was doing nothing but making me more tired, and showing God that I felt I could do more with my life than He could. Was God capable of running the ministry He had entrusted me with if I would just rest and trust in Him? Of course. Did He really *need* me to do all that I was doing? No.

"You're right, God, I'm *not* that important," I confessed aloud, right there on the rock on which I was sitting. "I don't have to be everywhere doing what ultimately only You can do. You are God and I am not. And I do want to find that resting place."

I still had to board a plane the next morning for my media tour. But while touring those cities, I sought out ways to rest and reflect on my relationship with God by taking long swims at the hotel pools, spending much time in prayer in my hotel rooms, and talking and listening to God during the long drives on the road. Upon arriving home three days later, I cleared my schedule by canceling a few speaking engagements and deciding *not* to do a number of things on my calendar that I had previously deemed necessary.

And I promised the Lord that from that day on, true rest and worship would be a priority in my life.

God has only blessed since.

God Commands Us to Rest

In Matthew 11:28, Jesus tells us to come to Him when we are weary and burnt out and He will give us rest.

"*This* is the resting place," Jesus is saying. "*I* am the resting place." To find true rest, we must get alone with God and turn things over to Him. God didn't merely suggest that to me that day when I was feeling overwhelmed. He was *commanding* it: *Cindi, slow down and quit trying to be everywhere and do everything as if everything depends on you. It doesn't. I will take care of all that concerns you; you just rest in Me.*

In Isaiah 28:12, when God lovingly urged His people to slow down by telling them, "This is the resting place," the people's tragic response to His command is stated in five very sad words: "*but they would not listen.*"

So God let them live an even more complicated, overwhelming, stress-inducing life: "So then, the word of the LORD to them will become: Do and do, do and do, rule on rule, rule on rule; a little here, a little there—so that they will go and fall backward, be injured and snared and captured" (Isaiah 28:13).

Our hopes of living freely and lightly certainly won't come by refusing to rest when God commands it. In fact, the opposite happens when we refuse to be obedient and rest: We become even more overwhelmed, more tired, more stressed—to the point of losing our health or becoming ensnared to the bondage of busyness. When God's people refused to obey God's command to rest, God eventually sent them into captivity for 70 years...one year for each Sabbath year (every seventh year) that the people had failed to honor a Sabbath rest for the land (2 Chronicles 36:20-21). They wouldn't obey God's command about rest, so their lives became more difficult and even more tiresome. God took it pretty seriously when His people refused to let the land rest. God called it sin.

This is the resting place...but they would not listen.

Will *you?*

Like a loving Father, God often does what's necessary to make us rest.

God Makes Us Rest

Any parent knows that without proper rest, his or her child will become unmanageable, unruly, unable to function. I remember those days when my two-year-old daughter skipped her afternoon nap. It wasn't a pretty picture. To this day, when she isn't in bed by a certain time, she becomes unreasonable. She simply can't function.

God knows we often react the same way. When we continue to go at a certain pace and don't slow down to rest or rejuvenate, we become unreasonable; we simply can't function in the way He created us to. Like children avoiding naptime, sometimes we even fight God because we don't want to *sit out* for awhile and rest.

So, like a loving Father, God often does what's necessary to *make* us rest. Just as a parent who puts a child to bed for his own good, our heavenly Father knows when it's time to make us rest.

For example, in Psalm 23:2, we're told that our loving Shepherd *makes* His sheep lie down in green pastures. Why does He make us rest? Because He knows we often won't do it on our own.

God has allowed (or perhaps resorted to!) a number of things in my own life to make me rest: a crashed computer so I can't work, a car in the shop that leaves me stranded at home for a few days, laryngitis so I can't speak for awhile, and the list goes on. He knows that sometimes He has to interrupt my schedule so I'm frustrated, feeling my hands are tied, and I can do nothing but lift my hands to Him and say "What? What do you want me to learn?" Often the answer is simply: "Nothing. I just want you to rest." At first, I concentrated on embracing those interruptions so God wouldn't have to take more drastic action to get my attention. But now I've decided it's a much smoother and wiser route to simply practice regular rest so God doesn't have to interrupt me in the first place to get me to be obedient and rest.

A friend, Tom, pastored a church in Colorado Springs for ten years. Every winter, he was snowed in for a few days and couldn't get his car onto the roads and had to stay home. He learned immediately to embrace those times of being snowed in by reading and writing letters by the fire while God breathed rest back into his life. He learned that at least once every winter, God *made* him lie down in snowy pastures. And he grew to appreciate—and long for—those times.

My friend Julie, an elementary-school teacher, tends to let her work life consume her. When she slipped in her garage and broke her right arm, she thought maybe God was trying to slow her down. But once she recovered, a basketball hit the back of her neck on the playground one afternoon, and she found herself flat on her back. Life had not just slowed down. It had come to a sudden halt.

On two different days, while taking MRIs to get at the root of why she couldn't move much or function in the way she had before, Julie was praying and both times heard God whisper to her heart, "Be still and know that I am God" (Psalm 46:10). She then realized God was wooing her back to a place where she would simply depend on Him and not stress over everything.

Once she recovered from the neck injury, she got right back into the throes of stress and anxiety on her job. Shortly afterward, she slipped in her garage and broke her *other* arm. Sudden halt again. By this time, Julie laughed at her situation and said "Do you think God might be trying to tell me something?"

I sympathize with Julie. I can't imagine being physically detained and having to move at a much slower pace. Yet I know my loving Father will do whatever it takes to make sure I'm living in a way that pleases Him. I don't want to be one whom God has to continually run after to get me to slow down. Oh, I want to be one who readily receives God's gift of rest so He doesn't have to do something drastic to get me flat on my back or to get me to slow down. Now, I'm not saying that every time we have a setback it means God is trying to get us to rest. But oftentimes that probably is the case. After all, He created us for the purpose of enjoying relationship with Him. And God will sometimes send us reminders to make sure we live out our purpose.

In Psalm 32:7, the psalmist sang, "God's my island hideaway; keeps danger far from the shore, throws garlands of hosannas around my neck" (THE MESSAGE). As I started thinking of God as my "island hideaway" I realized I can go away with Him in my heart every day…and find that place of rest and worship by sitting at His feet, being still in His presence, and letting His peace calm my heart. Even if I'm sitting at my desk at work, sitting in my car in traffic, or standing somewhere in line, I can find my island hideaway in Him and experience His "garland of rest" that He places warmly around my neck.

Receiving His Garland of Rest

Here are some practical ways to begin to embrace God's gift of rest.

1. Seek Out a Resting Place

Every woman needs her resting place—that place where she can sit back, close her eyes, and say, "Take me away, God, from the busyness of this moment, and help me find my stillness—and joy—in You." Ideally, that place is somewhere easily accessible where you can go every day. But if your routine is not the same every day, sometimes you must find that resting place wherever you go. When I take the train back to my hometown in Central California, my resting place is near the window, where I pray and write. When I am speaking at women's retreats, it is a quiet place in the woods, atop a rock, where I can breathe the mountain air and listen for His voice. When I'm at home, my resting place is on the floor of my study, early in the morning before anyone is up, where I sit backed up against the door and play worship music, sing to Him, and let Him unveil the riches of His character from His Word. Sometimes, in the stillness of the night, when my head is on my pillow and my mind is full of questions, my resting place is in Him, the only One who knows my heart and mind and has all the details of my life in His hands.

Where is *your* resting place? Could it be your back patio in the quiet of early morning or your living room chair after the kids leave for school? Perhaps it is your bedroom window just as the sun goes down. It might even be your car during your lunch hour at work or as you plan to arrive a half hour early to pick up your child or grandchild from school. Perhaps it may be your pillow each night as you reflect on Him before falling asleep. Begin thinking about where your resting place might be. If you can't find one, cry out to God to show you a place where You can meet Him in the quietness. I'm sure He's already chosen a place for the two of you; He's just been working on getting you there.

2. Sit in His Presence

Once you find your quiet place, go there regularly and just listen. It may take awhile for the noises around you and those incessant voices in your head to fade away. But listen, quiet your heart and mind. Write down distracting thoughts, if you must, with a pen and paper nearby. Then go back to sitting in the silence and focusing on God being there with you. Psalm 16:11 says, "You will fill me with joy in your presence." Experience the joy of just being in His presence…being still and being with Him. Remember, this time is not necessarily for you to hear something, get direction, and go on your way. This time is for you to just be together with God.

3. Set Your Mind on the Things Above

The Bible tells us to set our hearts and minds on things above where Christ is seated in heaven, "not on earthly things" (Colossians 3:1-2). It's so easy to get caught up with all we have to do here on earth and in our jobs and in our homes. But God wants us focused on the things of His kingdom…His holiness, our obedience, an eternal perspective about what matters and what doesn't. As you find your resting place and focus on God's presence, let Him take you to a place where your thoughts are no longer preoccupied with your list of things to do. Ask Him to help you slow down and notice the things He wants you to notice. Ask Him for a heavenly perspective, for a view of your life and all that you are doing from His vantage point. As you do this, you will find that your heart rate slows down a bit, and peace for the day floods your soul.

In Chapter 5, I will show you how to make searching the Scriptures and hearing from God a part of your quiet time with Him. But for now, learn how to sit with Him in the silence and set your mind on the things above, not the rat race here on earth.

Are You Ready to Rest?

As you seek out your resting place, sit in His presence, and set your mind and heart on the things above, you will be taking the first step in recovering your life. After all, as author John

Eldredge says, "The strategy of our enemy in the age we live in now is busyness or drivenness." Eldredge says the enemy's plan is this: "Keep them running, that way they'll never take care of their hearts. That way we'll burn them out, then take them out."[3]

But God has a better plan: "Get them resting in Me. That way their hearts will be in a place where I can minister to them and give them a zest for life that they never had before." By following God's call to be still, you are not only immunizing yourself against the enemy's attempts to burn you out, but you are opening the door to a multitude of blessings you will discover as you walk a slower path. And that, my friend, is what we'll look at next.

Carving Out Your "Rest Stops"

IN ORDER TO FIND REST FOR OUR SOULS, and not just for our minds and bodies, we must be right with God. We must know, for sure, that our soul is secure in God and that we have an eternal rest in our future. If you don't yet have the assurance that you have your eternal rest taken care of, you can be sure of that now, before going any further. Turn to page 177 at the end of the book and read through "Rest Assured." Then come back and continue on this journey with us.

1. Why do you think God *commands*, rather than suggests, we rest?

    If God suggest it will be one decision But if God commands the decision is already Made for us.

2. Reflect on the following verses and rewrite them here in your own words.

    Psalm 46:10— *Relax AND hear God*

    Psalm 62:1— *Have patience aND God will come thru*

    Psalm 91:1— *Hide yourself aND LeT God be seen*

    Psalm 107:29-30— *He brings peACE, When things ARE shakey, Then you are settled*

3. In what way might God be saying to you, "This is the resting place, let the weary rest"?

I am hERE iN SC with No family.

Write out your response to God's command for you to rest:

You Know what LorD I needed a rest from my situations not a rest from. I seem and feel so useless. But I know this is a way that you wanted me to go.

4. Write one place that you can retreat to—every day—that will allow you to get quiet and alone with God (even if just for a few moments) and regain your rest. Be creative with this—your car, your closet, or the corner of your backyard are options, too.

My daily resting place: *bathroom*

If you look at the world, you'll be distressed. If you look within, you'll be depressed. But if you look at Christ, you'll be at rest!

CORRIE TEN BOOM

Two

Finding Soothing Waters
on a Slower Path

STARING OUT THE CAR WINDOW at the rolling grasslands of northeastern Ohio, I was amazed. This California native had never seen such expanse in her entire life. There was a peace and a quiet to that open space. A hush came over me as I passed wide-open fields of wheat. Out here in the heart of Amish country, there existed a slower pace of life…and it called to me.

I was en route to a beautiful Amish inn where I was to speak for a women's retreat. By the time I arrived, I was already inspired by the quiet country life and the occasional old-fashioned buggy that rolled by. But when I was shown to my "executive suite" where I would be staying for the weekend, it was the Jacuzzi bathtub that I knew would do the trick.

The beautiful tub, enclosed by curtains with greenery and silk flowers cascading down both sides, called to me for an evening of rest and relaxation. But wanting to savor the experience, I decided to schedule a bubble bath in the tub after my presentation on Saturday evening, when I typically tend to be the most exhausted. So, after my talk, I settled into my room for the night, filled up the tub, poured in the gel bubble bath that the host church had given me, got a book to read, and then settled into the water for my evening of relaxation. I reached behind me to turn on the jets and…WHOOSH! Like a scene out of *I Love Lucy!* water pelted me from every direction with the force of four giant fire hoses as I screamed and fumbled behind me to turn off the jets. White foamy bubbles and water sprayed all over the bathroom, soaking the curtains and knocking down the cascading flower arrangements. By the time I got the jets turned off, the entire bathroom was a bubbly, soaking mess. I sat there for a moment, stunned at the experience. Disgusted, I picked up my sopping-wet book, reached for a drenched towel, and stepped out of the tub. So much for the restful experience!

> *I* was looking for a change of location to bring me rest. What I really needed was a change of lifestyle.

As I caught my reflection in the mirror—showing a heap of bubbles and silk flowers on my head, as well as mascara smeared all over my eyes—I had to laugh. *Cindi, this is what you get for looking to something the world has to offer for your rest and relaxation,* I thought. I realized then that I was given a visual example of how frustrated we can become when we look to something from this world for our rest and discover it doesn't work!

Our Great Escapes

Women are great at planning "escapes." While God woos us to come away with Him, we instead look for other ways to find peace and rest. We search for an escape in chocolate, shopping trips, bubble baths, or a massage. We dream about (and possibly even go on) vacations to faraway paradises like Hawaii, where we figure our hearts and minds will be restored. But after some temporary relaxation, has anything about the stress and pace of our life really changed?

I recently went with my husband and daughter on a family-oriented cruise to the Bahamas and spent a day on a white sand beach. For weeks I talked of the "rest" I would receive while on the cruise ship, while sunning in the Bahamas, while laying around the pool deck on the ship. But I found, instead, that there was so much to *do* on the ship, so many things to *see* as we pulled into an exotic port, that the rest never came. In fact, I came home more tired than I was when I left. I was looking for a change of *location* to bring me rest. What I really needed was a change of *lifestyle*.

God spoke to His people repeatedly about their need for a change in their lifestyle. With rebellious hearts that insisted they didn't need God, the Israelites pursued cheap substitutes for God and continually experienced frustration, punishment, and bondage because of it. Angered by their rebellion, God said in Jeremiah 2:13 that His people had "forsaken me, the spring of living water, and have dug their own cisterns, broken cisterns that cannot hold water."

Does that sound like us sometimes? Do we refuse to go to God, our Living Water, when we need refreshment, insisting we can find it somewhere else? Do we continually look to the world for a slice of rest, when God's Word says, "My soul finds rest in God alone" (Psalm 62:1)? I know I sometimes do. And the moment we find ourselves in need of something (in this case, rest) and we are tempted to look somewhere else to fill that need, we find ourselves at a crossroads. What will we do? Where will we go? Which direction will we turn for our answer? God clearly told His people what to do when they were at a crossroads. I believe His instruction is worth heeding today: "Stand at the crossroads and look; ask for the ancient paths, ask where the good way is, and walk in it, and you will find rest for your souls" (Jeremiah 6:16).

When we are at a crossroads, wondering how to proceed, we are told to ask God for the "ancient paths," and therein we will find rest.

Echoes of the Ancient Path

I've been thinking a lot lately about what it means to take the "ancient path." Could that be the path Enoch took when he walked with God 300 years (Genesis 5:23-24)? If so, it would be a path of taking the time to walk and talk with God, to connect with His heart, to know what He wants of me. Could it be the path Abraham chose when God called him His friend (Isaiah 41:8)? If so, that would be the path of obedience, of going out not knowing where we're going, simply because God told us to. A life of faith and trust, where we can't see where God might be leading, but we're placing ourselves in the hands of God who *can* see all things perfectly. Or could it be the path David took when he said, "My soul finds rest in God alone" (Psalm 62:1)? David often rose early in the morning and waited for God "more than watchmen wait for the morning" (Psalm 130:6).

Each of those portraits shows me a life that knew of rest, waiting, and peace. A life of relationship. A life in which these individuals abided in God, as we should. I'm beginning to think that taking an ancient path means walking a route that has long been forgotten, taking the path less traveled. Sometimes older paths are more difficult to walk, but they are simpler, and they lead straight to God's heart.

When God said, "Ask for the ancient paths," He was, in a sense, saying, "Go back to the old ways, when life was simple." And those old ways might be slower ways, but they will take us to Him, whereas the newer ways will take us straight to the distractions that have led so many of us to a life of feeling over-whelmed. I believe God was saying, "Walk the slower path, the one on which you commune with Me the whole way, the one on which you enjoy My presence along the way, the path that leads straight to My heart."

Taking Time to Be "Schooled"

I was encouraged one morning when my husband preached about being "schooled" in the discipline of silence. He shared with us that the word *school* literally means "free time." And to be *schooled* by someone meant we spent much free time with them, sitting at their feet, learning of them, being mentored in their ways. He then pointed out the story in Luke 24:13-32 about the two men who walked with Jesus shortly after Jesus' resurrec-tion from the dead, but at first didn't recognize it was Jesus who was beside them. The two men were simply discussing the many things they had questions about when a stranger met them on the road and said, "What are you discussing together as you walk along?" (verse 17). The two were surprised to hear the stranger asking about what everyone knew as they talked. Then Jesus explained to them, going from one end of the Bible to the other, everything said in Scripture about Jesus and how it was fulfilled. Later, He vanished from their sight. It was then the men real-ized they had literally had the Word of God in their midst. They were being "schooled" in the Scriptures by the Author of the Scriptures Himself. Their response, upon realizing this, was, "Were not our hearts burning within us while he talked with us on the road and opened the Scriptures to us?" (verse 32).

What do you suppose would have happened if these two men had been in too much of a hurry to slow down and listen to that "stranger" on the road that day? What if they had worried about their schedule and said, "We're sorry, sir, we don't have time to talk right now," and rushed off? What they would've missed!

I put myself in that picture and wonder if I would've slowed down to be "schooled in the Scriptures" with Jesus. Or, would I have rushed by, considering my schedule and all the things I'm doing for God more important than actually being with God Himself? Would I have been too set in my way and too harried to stop for a moment that was holy? Those two men, fortunately, chose the ancient path of taking the time to be schooled in the wisdom and knowledge of the Scriptures from the Author of Scripture. What a once-in-a-lifetime opportunity! They certainly experienced the reward of walking an ancient path.

I have found that when I slow down to take the ancient path, I end up experiencing many blessings I would've otherwise missed.

My Trek on an Ancient Path

One morning while I was at a conference, my mind was bogged down with a situation in my marriage. I was basically mad at Hugh for not spending the time with me that I had desired before I left for the conference. And I wanted him to call and repent. I also wanted to not forgive him if he did make the call. (I know, pretty evil, huh?) I knew my thinking was wrong, but I didn't want to give in this time. The morning session was starting, but as I walked there, my heart became heavier and heavier. I could literally feel God pulling at my heart as if to say, "Come away with Me...let's talk about this...let's make this right...now!"

I skipped the session and found a quiet corner in the convention center. I poured out my heart to God and He brought me to the story of Abraham and the ancient path he took. Abraham climbed up Mount Moriah to offer to God his son, whom he loved. Abraham did it because he trusted God when God asked him for the sacrifice.

"Do *you* trust Me?" God seemed to be saying to me as He urged me to walk up Mount Moriah and there offer Him what I had been holding onto. "Yes..." I whispered to Him. I looked again at the story and found that as Abraham obediently offered what he loved the most to God, God intervened and provided a different sacrifice altogether. And there was joy that followed.

I offered to God—again—my marriage, my perceived rights, my expectations, and my stubbornness to hold onto the situation and said, "I trust You...that You will provide." That evening, the woman who had organized the conference and was staying in the executive suite came up to me and handed me her room key. She said, "I get the room for one more night after the convention ends as a thank-you from the hotel, but God kept insisting I give it to you. Call your husband and tell him God has arranged for the two of you to have some time together." She didn't know a thing about what I wrestled with that morning... but when I walked down that ancient path and was willing to give up what I felt I needed with my husband, God had clearly provided in an unexpected way. Hugh met me there at the hotel that evening and we took a swim in the pool and had a special time of talking and healing...and joy followed. When I tried to work it all out myself, I was tired, frustrated, and discouraged. When I offered it to God, arms wide open, He took the burden and provided for me in unexpected ways. He gave to me out of His abundance what I couldn't have found out of the feebleness of my own striving.

It's clear that the path the world is taking to find rest involves quick, easy ways to find "sudden relief." But God says, "Come away with Me. Let's talk. Get it off your mind and hand it over to Me so I can carry it for you...then you will learn of Me and you can live lightly and freely."

Rest isn't just laying down and clearing your mind. It's retraining your mind to turn over the problems to the only One who is able to work them all out. And as we hand them all over to Him, He leaves us with minds at peace and arms that are no longer overloaded.

The ancient path Jesus offers is one in which we spend our free time being schooled in the presence of Jesus. A time in which we come away saying, "Didn't my heart burn within me as I stood in His presence, as I sensed His direction from His Word, as I walked with Him on the ancient path?"

Refusing to Run on the Harried Path

I find it interesting that in Scripture, God never tells His people, "Hurry up, get going, faster!" No, those are words I often say to my daughter as we're rushing out the door or rushing around town. But God's words, instead, are, "Be still." "Wait." "Rest." The holy path is one that will take time to walk. It will involve waiting. It will involve trusting. But it will be peaceful, and you will find rest for your soul. The harried path, on the other hand, is one that is quick as lightning. It is one that everyone is running upon. But it leaves you run-down, exhausted, and overwhelmed. Which path would *you* rather take?

The harried path offers rushing waters and Jacuzzi jets that are out of control. The ancient path leads to soothing waters that refresh us. In Psalm 23:2, David says our Good Shepherd leads us "beside quiet waters"—the soothing, still waters of His refreshment, not the rushing rivers the world has to offer.

What are the soothing waters God leads us beside?

- A peace that passes understanding (Philippians 4:7).

- An assurance that He is in control (Psalm 46:10).

- A wisdom that is beyond this world—the kind of wisdom that takes time to develop.

- An authenticity and a deeper life—one in which we can reflect on what we did yesterday and learn from it.

One of the rewards of walking the slower path is becoming a more authentic and a deeper Christian:

> Authentic Christians are persons who stand apart from others, even other Christians, as though listening to a different drummer. Their character seems deeper, their ideas fresher, their spirit softer, their courage greater, their

leadership stronger, their concerns wider, their compassion more genuine, their convictions more concrete. They are joyful in spite of difficult circumstances and show wisdom beyond their years....That's because authentic Christians have strong relationships with the Lord—relationships that are renewed every day.

Embarrassingly few Christians ever reach this level of authenticity; most Christians are just too busy. And the archenemy of spiritual authenticity is busyness, which is closely tied to something the Bible calls *worldliness*—getting caught up with this society's agenda, objectives and activities to the neglect of walking with God.

Any way you cut it, a key ingredient in authentic Christianity is time. Not leftover time, not throwaway time, but quality time. Time for contemplation, meditation and reflection. Unhurried, uninterrupted time.[1]

"Deep calls to deep," the psalmist says in Psalm 42:7. As we slow down to hear God's call on our life, we can go deeper with Him. When we're going too fast to listen, we will live in the illusion that we're okay—even if we're painfully complacent.

What About You?

Isn't it about time you take that ancient path and find the soothing waters of rest and refreshment along the way? It all happens when you stand at the crossroads and look and say, "From this day forward, I'm going to choose the path less traveled...the one that leads straight to my Father's heart. I'm going to walk a bit slower if it means walking with Him."

Do it, and you *will* find rest for your soul.

Stopping Beside Quiet Waters

Which of the following represents the ancient path as opposed to today's path of hurriedness? (Circle the words that describe the ancient path.)

Emailing a quick note to a friend	OR	Sending a handwritten card to someone who needs encouragement
Driving to the quick-mart	OR	Walking a few blocks to the store and taking in all you never noticed before
Reading a one-minute devotional for your morning quiet time	OR	Spending some time with just your Bible and a journal
Talking to God "on the fly"	OR	Communing deeply with God in a quiet room

Think of your daily routine. Now, write out a few of your regular activities, first recording what you do, then thinking of a way you can do the same activity by taking the ancient path.

This may include even simple actions such as taking time to say hi to someone along the way. As you think of ways to slow down, you may find a number of ways you can make life more meaningful.

What comes to your mind when you think of soothing waters? List your thoughts here. Then ask God to help you make these part of your life.

_____

_____

_____

_____

_____

_____

Whenever anything begins to disintegrate your life with Jesus Christ, turn to Him at once and ask Him to establish rest.

OSWALD CHAMBERS

THREE

Focusing on the
Few Things That Matter

SITTING AT THE TABLE WITH MY FRIEND, Edie, I was instantly convicted. This cancer survivor had put her priorities in order years before when she realized she may have less time to live than she thought. When she asked me the riveting question, I felt uncomfortable:

"Cindi, why are you in such a hurry?" Edie asked. Before I could respond, she continued: "You're young. You can do what you're doing for another 20 years after your daughter is grown and leaves for college, but you have only so much time left with her while she's still a child and at home. Savor this time with her. You'll never get back her little girl years."

Edie was so right. And I have never regretted the decision I made that very same day to clear my calendar and reprioritize my life so I could savor Dana's little-girl years.

I guess I had to hear it from a cancer survivor.

I've often wondered how radically my life might change if I were to hear that I suddenly had a lot less time to live than I thought. Seriously, if I were diagnosed with cancer and told I had six to eight months to live, would I live differently? You bet! I'm sure I would...

- Spend quality time every day with my husband and daughter

- Cut out the busy work at home and church

- Write more letters (old-fashioned letters, not emails) to my family and closest friends

- Spend more time in heart preparation every day

- Spend longer, richer times in worship

- Enjoy a sunset, walk in the sun, climb a mountain, take more prayer walks

In other words, I would instantly make sure the things that are eternal (people I love, God, anything done for Him) preoccupied my time. I wouldn't waste a day worrying or striving for something that was beyond my control. I'd instead relish each breath, cherish each day, and make sure I loved and lived to the fullest before each sundown.

So, why am I not living that way now?

If you really think about it, none of us knows exactly when our last day on this earth will be. I may be living today with a condition or diagnosis I know nothing about. Or, my time, or yours, may be up in a car accident tomorrow. We just don't know. But the Bible tells us our days *are* numbered (Psalm 139:16), and therefore, we all have limited time left to make an impact on this earth.

The psalm writer said, "Teach us to number our days aright, that we may gain a heart of wisdom" (Psalm 90:12). God has already numbered our days, and in some cases, He allows us to know when our end is coming close so we can be careful to live those last few days or weeks or months wisely. But most of us have no idea when we will draw our last breath. So, with that in mind, asking God to help us number our days, or be aware that our lives will someday come to an end, is one way of saying, "Lord, help me live in a way that counts. Give me discernment to know what will last and what will not so I can live wisely." What better way to practice a lifestyle of rest than to live lightly and freely as if we had not much time left!

I'm sure you've heard the stories or read the emails of the old woman, lying on her deathbed, talking of her regrets. She wishes she'd used her special china more frequently, gone barefoot in the grass more often, taken more risks, helped more people, loved more selflessly, and spent more time with her children. The list goes on. To number our days, or live as if they're numbered, is to recognize what is most important from day to day and to make the most of each moment.

Jesus Numbered His Days

Jesus knew when He walked this earth that His days were numbered. Being God in the flesh, He knew that at the age of 33 He would give His life as a ransom for the sins of mankind. So He didn't waste any time doing things that held no eternal value or weren't part of His mission here on earth. We don't read of Him spending hours or days worrying about matters such as His impending death or how He was going to get His disciples into tip-top faith shape by the time He left this earth. Instead, He instructed others, "Do not worry about your life...or about your body....Who of you by worrying can add a single hour to his life? And why do you worry about clothes?....Therefore do not worry about tomorrow...."[1] We don't read about Jesus' regrets—He didn't have any because He was careful to consult His Father before He did anything. We don't read about Him becoming frustrated with so many people to heal, so many thousands to feed, so many sermons to give, because Jesus knew the one thing He was here for: to do His Father's will. He healed, fed, and taught as His Father led Him—and did no more, no less.

Jesus' words to His Father in His prayer in John 17 set an example for us to follow: "I have finished the work which You have given Me to do" (verse 4 NKJV). That's our only responsibility, isn't it? To finish the work *He* gives us. Not all the things we expect ourselves to do. Not all the things others expect us to accomplish. But only the things *He* gives us to do. What are those things?

> *It's much harder to follow God's call if I'm running too fast to hear Him speak.*

- Love the Lord your God with all your heart, soul, mind, and strength (Matthew 22:37).

- Love your neighbor as yourself (Matthew 22:39).

- Act justly, love mercy, and walk humbly with your God (Micah 6:8).

- Be still and know that He is God (Psalm 46:10).

Exchanging the Burden

No wonder Jesus encouraged us in Matthew 11:28-30 to come to Him and lay down our heavy burdens and pick up His instead. Our burdens are weighty—all those things we feel we must do for ourselves, for others, and for God. Yet Jesus says His burden is light. What burden does He place upon us? Those I just listed. The burden to love Him with all our hearts, to love others more than ourselves, to walk humbly, to rest. No, His burdens are not heavy. Ours are. So it's time to lay them down and focus on the few things that really matter. And that means focusing on only what God requires of us, and that is often far less than we are requiring of ourselves.

I realized recently that I'm busy because I *do* things for God (many of which He hasn't necessarily asked me to do), not because I'm just *being* with Him. Yet God doesn't want me to just do things *for* Him. He wants me to be *with* Him. He wants the relationship. As I grow to love Him, I will want to serve Him. My work will flow from my worship. My labor for Him will stem from my love for Him. He knows that. So He wants us to work on the relationship first. Once the work takes priority in our lives, He knows the relationship will go downhill. And He's willing to do what it takes to keep that from happening. It's much harder to follow God's call if I'm running too fast to hear Him speak. And I'm realizing, as well, that when I slow down, I'm not missing anything. I'm actually putting myself in the place where I'll receive a lot more—much more than if I were running quickly to get all I was trying to get for myself.

A Tale of Two Sisters

Do you ever wonder if someday you'll have a chance to look back upon your life on this earth and see what the most important moments were and whether you seized them or let them slip away? I believe Jesus gave us a story of an incident that occurred in His life so that we won't make the same mistake that one busy, distracted, striving woman made…and miss the moments when we could have slowed down and enjoyed being with Him. I think He gave us this story so we would know how to number our days.

Jesus and His disciples stopped by the home of Martha and her sister, Mary, in Bethany one day to rest and eat. But when the entourage of men with dirty feet and hungry stomachs stopped by, Martha must have realized there was much to do to make their stay a comfortable one. Or was there?

Martha, the older sister and presumably the most responsible, got to work setting the table, figuring out where she was going to put all the guests, planning the menu, cooking the food, all the while directing people here and there. What a multitasking woman! I imagine she was delegating duties to the servants and proving herself a top administrator! But something was not going according to plan. *Where was Mary?*

Martha became irritated when she noticed that her sister, who should've been alongside her carrying out her orders, was instead in the living room with the men, sitting on her duff and listening to Jesus.

Annoyed, perhaps even enraged, that her sister would leave her to do all the work, Martha insisted that Jesus come to her aid: "Lord, doesn't it seem unfair to you that my sister just sits here while I do all the work? Tell her to come and help me," she complained (Luke 10:40 NLT).

Oh, how we wish the next line read, "And Jesus turned a glaring eye to Mary and said 'Get in the kitchen and help your sister. Who are you to sit it out when there's work to be done?'"

I tend to think we wish Jesus had made such a statement because then all of us workhorses would be justified for all the work we *do*. And all those women at church who seem to be sitting around would no longer have an excuse!

But Jesus didn't see the situation the way Martha did. Nor does He see circumstances the way we often do. He wasn't concerned with everything this woman-in-charge thought needed to be done. He knew a more important, life-changing opportunity was at hand. God in the flesh was in their living room imparting words of wisdom. And Martha was missing it!

Rather than insisting that Mary get up and help her sister, Jesus gently rebuked Martha for not having the quiet heart Mary was displaying.

"Martha," Jesus answered. "You are so upset over all these details! There is really only one thing worth being concerned about. Mary has discovered it—and I won't take it away from her."[2]

Was Jesus saying Martha's work wasn't important? No. He said that "all these details" were not worthy of her concern. Yes, they eventually needed to eat, but they didn't need matching plates and ornamental candleholders and a centerpiece that would be the talk of the town. They didn't need everything to be in perfect order. They didn't need the women to make a fuss. And besides, wasn't the One who turned five loaves of bread and two fish into a dinner for more than 5,000 sitting in their midst? Surely He could handle matters if Martha couldn't get it all done. But most of all, I think, Jesus was trying to show Martha that while she scampered about the kitchen preparing the food, the Bread of Life[3] was already in her living room. Jesus wanted this woman to see that when God is in her midst, nothing is more important than revering Him. He wanted her to know this was a life-changing encounter—one she shouldn't miss.

Likewise, the Lord wants *us* to know when to stop doing all that the world says we must do and instead, take time to simply sit at the feet of the King of Glory. And when we do, we can leave that encounter a changed person who possesses something that can never be taken from us. The food Martha prepared that night was eventually eaten and then gone forever. But what Mary fed upon at the feet of Jesus would remain in her heart and could never be taken away.

In Jesus' rebuke to Martha in Scripture, I hear Him rebuking me as well: "Cindi, Cindi, why do you run around doing so many things? I am not impressed with all your busyness, but only with the time you spend with Me. Can you give up what the world says you must do in order to sit at My feet and learn of Me?"

Oh, how I long for my response to be, "Yes, Lord, I will let these distractions fall by the wayside so I can spend more time at Your feet. Eliminate my fear of disappointing people, and my fear of appearing weak or unable, and replace them with a wholesome fear of disappointing *You*."

I truly want Jesus to say about me someday the same statement Jesus made about Mary—that I had discovered the "one thing" that couldn't be taken from me.

Grasping the "One Thing"

What *is* the "one thing" Jesus referred to? I believe it was sitting at Jesus' feet, seizing the time to be with Him and Him alone, realizing that the moment He was in the living room might never come again and grabbing hold of it so it could be relished forever.

In Psalm 27:4, David said, "The *one thing* I ask of the LORD— the *one thing* I seek most—is to live in the house of the LORD all the days of my life, delighting in the Lord's perfections and meditating in His Temple" (NLT).

David knew the one thing He wanted. It was to be in God's presence. Abiding with Him. Dwelling with Him. Making his home with Him. Mary apparently wanted that one thing as well, for she sat at Jesus' feet to soak up all He had to say.

Jesus wants us to grab hold of the *one thing* that matters, too: dwelling in His presence. Yes, He desires that we tell others about Him, that we be connected to one another as we serve in the church to build up the body, that we boldly proclaim who He is. But we can't do any of that effectively and sincerely if we don't truly know Him. And that comes from being in His presence and sitting at His feet as Mary did. Our work for Him must flow from our worship of Him. Our labor for Him must be an outpouring of our love for Him. So being with Him to cultivate that love relationship is imperative.

You and I were created to love God and enjoy Him forever. If His purpose for us were to just accomplish things for Him, then His greatest commandment for us would have clearly stated the work we are to *do*. Yet God's greatest commandment, recorded in Matthew 22:37-38, is that we *love* Him with all our heart, soul, mind, and strength! God knows that if we love Him above all else, we'll have no problem obeying Him and doing anything He asks of us. How wonderfully freeing! To know that this God who loves us and wants to enjoy us commands that our first priority in life—the one thing we do above all else—is to *love Him*. What an incredible thought!

Dismissing the Distractions

Yet as Martha showed us, the spur-of-the-moment distractions, the call from the kitchen, the list of things to do keeps us from sitting at His feet, being with Him, worshiping Him, resting in Him. Our busyness robs us of giving to Jesus the one thing He truly desires.

I love the fact that Mary was so immersed in Jesus' teaching that she apparently was oblivious to Martha's state of frustration. We don't read that Mary got up and apologized to Martha, or started feeling guilty, or ran out of the room, crying at being singled out for not helping. Mary was so wrapped up in Jesus she didn't notice the commotion her absence from the kitchen had caused. Oh, to be so immersed in Jesus that you and I are oblivious to the self-induced frustrations of every stressed-out person in this world! That is truly living—and resting—as if our days are numbered.

Now, this is not to say that taking care of our household responsibilities isn't important. We do have obligations to care for our husband, children, ourselves, and our guests. Scripture does call us to be hospitable, to serve, and to care for others. That's all part of the Christian life. But we should make sure that in fulfilling our daily priorities we don't sacrifice the one true priority—seeking time alone with God.

Ways to Number Our Days

So how can you and I maintain the right priorities at the right time so we are free to focus on the few things that reallly matter?

1. Practice the Presence of God

I mentioned in chapter 1 the importance of seeking out a quiet place and sitting in the presence of God. Once you're doing that, you're ready to go a bit deeper. A key part of numbering your days means you will make each one on earth a special memory with Jesus. To do that, you have to carve out time to sit before Him alone, whether by playing a worship CD and just thinking of Him, by taking a walk with Him and listening to what He says to your heart, or by reading aloud His Word and praying it back to Him in adoration, praise, and thanksgiving. You and I want to be in "worship shape" when we come before God's throne someday. Imagine entering heaven and feeling so at home in the presence of God that eternity is, for you, a glorious extension of the personal devotional life you cultivated here on earth. To number our days is to prepare our hearts for home through worship.

I did that recently while at a beach. My church had come together for a time of fellowship and baptisms, but while people were still gathering I wandered over to a pile of rocks near the shore. It was one of those snapshot moments when I was wanting to talk to the Creator of the beauty around me. I climbed onto one of the rocks and began to praise God for what He had made and what He was doing in my life. I then thought about the span of my life, as seen through God's eyes. What would stand out the most when my life rolled out before Him? What snapshots would summarize how I spent most of my time on this earth? I then prayed a simple prayer: "Lord, when You go through the snapshots of my life, I want the worship times to outweigh the frantic times. I want times of reflection to outnumber times of busyness. And I long for my life to be more holy than harried, be more rested than rushed, and to involve far more times of praise for You than public performance by me." I realized then that I wanted moments like those—of sitting on the rocks at the beach, talking to Him—to be a pattern in my life. "Lord, may these special times of being alone with you be among the defining times of my life, so I am remembered by You and others not as one 'who never had time' but as one 'who always made time' to be with You."

I walked away from there thinking that if I only had a few short weeks to live, that is one of the things I would have done...and would do again. One way to number our days is to offer up meaningful snapshots to God of moments in our life when we grabbed hold of perspective and recommitted ourselves to loving Him and serving Him more fully.

2. Prioritize People over Productivity

To number my days also means prioritizing people in my life. As I'm spending adequate time with God, He'll give back to me that time to spend with those whom I love. And I've found that God's peace comes when we reprioritize our lives in such a way that God and others whom we love are not cheated out of the time they deserve.

In his book *Choosing to Cheat: Who Wins When Family and Work Collide?* author Andy Stanley says, "...when we are willing to reprioritize in a way that honors our heavenly Father, He is willing to touch down in the midst of our personal chaos and bring the order and balance we so desperately desire."[4]

I recently noticed how much my daughter was missing in life because her mom was so busy. "Do I have to constantly rearrange my life for your schedule?" I selfishly blurted out to her one afternoon as she complained about me not being able to come back to the school and pick her up again if she stayed to watch a basketball game. Then pain pulsed through my heart as I realized *I* was the one who was selfishly rearranging *her* life to fit within *my* schedule. I blew off the rest of the things I had hoped to get done that day and stayed and watched the basketball game with her at school. Then we came home and I made her favorite macaroni and cheese for dinner. It was nothing super self-sacrificial on my part. It was, after all, what mothers do—cook for their kids and spend time with them. I had just finally realized that ten years from that day, or sometime after I'm dead and gone, nothing I would've done that day (from my "to do list") would've been remembered by my daughter. But she *would* remember me going to a basketball game with her and blowing off the rest of the day so we could be together.

I'm finding that David's prayer in Psalm 90:12—in which he asks God to teach us to number our days—means, "Teach us how to know the difference between what will last and what will not and help us spend our time accordingly." Time spent extending one's self toward others and building into their lives is one of those things that will last.

3. *Pursue Moments of Joy*

One of my "joy moments"—a snapshot in my life in which I felt near to heaven—was one Saturday afternoon at Wonder Valley in Central California. I was speaking at a retreat, and the warm weather in early March made my heart sing. I asked a woman if I could borrow her bicycle and I sped along a path with rolling green hills and trees surrounding me. It was breathtakingly beautiful and refreshingly simple. A childhood pleasure like riding a bike became a worship moment for me, with the wind in my face, the sun on my back, and a heart full of praise and gratitude that I was alive. It was this kind of moment that I definitely need more of if I'm going to number my days.

What are some "joy moments" you can live out? Think of what you can do to stir up joy in your heart, a smile on your face, and praise on your lips. Then experience those moments with God!

Let the Countdown Begin

This is where it starts, my friend. You're on your way to living differently from this day forward by focusing on the few things that really matter. So, let the countdown begin...and be encouraged that as God teaches you to number your days, you will be able to present back to Him a heart of wisdom—a heart that is focused on the one thing He desires of you...your love and rest in Him.

$\mathcal{F}$ocusing on the One Thing

List five things you would change or do differently if you discovered you had only six months to live:

1.

2.

3.

4.

5.

Pray right now and ask God for the ability to live this way *today*. You may want to take one item on your list and focus on doing it until it becomes routine, and then move on to the next one. (Remember, if time were short, the motivation *would* be there. Then consider this: None of us knows how short our time really is.)

What is the "one thing" you believe God is calling you to do in order to keep His greatest commandment (Matthew 22:37-38)?

Ask God now to help you focus on that "one thing."

Write Psalm 90:12 here and commit it to memory. This verse will serve as a great reminder to you of your need for rest.

*O*h, beloved, we want to realize that it is just on account of there being so much of that self-life in us that the power of God cannot work in us as mightily as God is willing that it should work.

ANDREW MURRAY

If we want to earn glory, we must flee from human glory and only desire glory from God. Then we will obtain and enjoy both through the grace and loving-kindness of our Lord Jesus Christ.

CHRYSOSTOM

FOUR

Surrendering the Need to Succeed

THE DAY I CLEARED MY CALENDAR and decided to quit striving and start focusing on the few things that matter, fear shot through me momentarily.

What if by backing off from my speaking schedule I begin to lose all I've worked for? What if it appears I am giving up? What if my life and work fall apart around me because I'm not working as hard as I used to? What if it looks like I'm being lazy? What if no one else understands?

And then the Spirit of God calmed my heart: *Cindi, would I ask you to do something to please My heart and then punish you for being obedient? Trust Me.*

I did.

Then I got a call from my editor.

"Cindi, what have you been up to the past month?" he asked. My first thought was: *He knows! He's probably seen the sales figures on my books and has figured out I've been doing nothing. After all, if most authors aren't out there speaking, their books are not selling.*

"Well," I explained, "I've been convicted about the busyness in my life and felt I needed to reprioritize and make some changes in how I've been living. So I've been spending more time at home with my husband and daughter, spending more time in my church on Sundays—instead of being out there speaking every weekend—and doing a lot of praying and waiting on the Lord. I just felt I needed to trust Him with my ministry instead of thinking I had to do it all myself." And then I added, almost apologetically, "I guess I've been doing a whole lot of what probably looks to you guys like nothing."

"Well, I guess God is confirming what you really should be doing," my editor replied. When I asked him to explain, he said that in the past month, when I had been simply resting and trusting, my book sales had doubled over the previous month's sales. And in the first four months of the year, my second book had outsold what my first book had sold over a period of two years.

My editor wasn't calling to tell me to work harder or hang it up. He was simply asking how I was doing and wanted to let me know the book was doing well. And in reality, I'd been doing nothing to make the book do well except obeying God's call to rest and trust in Him. God was doing it all. And my editor's call that day not only convinced me that God wanted me to continue in this lifestyle of rest, but it affirmed to me that my God could do more with my ministry in two months than I could do with it in two years!

With a return like that, why *wouldn't* we want to place everything we do in God's hands and let Him do what He can do so much better than us?

The Secret to Our Success

Striving is one of the reasons we don't rest. It is what had me continually uptight about where I should be and how I was supposed to get there. We want to be the best at what we do—as wives, mothers, career women, and servants of God. Yet Psalm 138:8 says, "The LORD will accomplish what concerns me" (NASB). He, too, wants us to be the best wives, mothers, workers, and servants that we can be, which is why He wants us to rest in Him, rely on Him, and allow Him to do through us what only He can do.

In John 15:5, Jesus said, "I am the vine; you are the branches. If a man remains in me and I in him, he will bear much fruit; apart from me you can do nothing." That sure is true in my life. When I try to do things in my own way, at my own speed, I never seem to get much accomplished. But as I abide in Him, He causes me to be far more productive than I could be apart from Him. From a human perspective this may not make sense, but it's one of those ways of God that we don't quite understand (Isaiah 55:8-9). That is the secret to our success. To remain in Him, consider a relationship with Him of utmost priority, "and all these things will be given to you" (Matthew 6:33).

When we surrender our need to succeed and come to God and say, "I just need *You*," we are then in a position to succeed no matter what. God promises in His Word that when we seek Him we will find Him when we search for Him with all our hearts (Jeremiah 29:13). He tells us when we seek first His kingdom, all the problems and needs of life we tend to worry about will fall into place (Matthew 6:33). He tells us that when we delight ourselves in Him, by having a desire for Him only, He will give us the desires of our hearts (Psalm 37:4). I'm not saying put God first and He'll make only good things happen in your life. I'm saying put Him first, rely on Him, seek only Him, and He will satisfy you in the search. He will become the One you desire and therefore you will have all you want and need.

God's Success Search

In 2 Chronicles 16:9, we discover that "the eyes of the LORD move to and fro throughout the earth that He may strongly support those whose heart is completely His" (NASB). God is looking for those who are fully depending on Him, obeying Him, and resting in Him so He can bless all they put their hand to. Do you see the irony in this principle of God's? Rather than striving, if we begin trusting and resting, God will see to it that we succeed. We find this principle elsewhere in the Bible, too. We find in Psalm 1:1-3 that the person who delights in God's Word will yield fruit in season and "in whatever he does, he prospers." Likewise, in Jeremiah 17:7-8, we find that those who trust in the Lord and put their confidence in Him (instead of in ourselves and how hard we work, or how fast we run) "are not bothered by the heat or worried by long months of drought. Their leaves stay green, and they go right on producing delicious fruit" (NLT).

> *He tells us to leave behind the striving and the stress that accompanies it, and wait on Him.*

Abandoning the Ambition

I wonder if one reason we run ourselves ragged is because we follow our own ambitions. We run so hard after certain goals or pursuits that we fail to see the absurdity—and uselessness—of doing so.

My friend Paul and I were talking recently about the dangers of pride, which accompanies the drive to succeed. He made a comment that has stuck with me since our conversation. He said, "God begins to work in our life when the ambitions are gone." I've thought long and hard about that. When my ambition is for self gain, there is no room for God. But when my goal is like that of Paul my friend and Paul the apostle—"to know [Christ] and the power of his resurrection and the fellowship of sharing in his sufferings" (Philippians 3:10)—then God will do a work in me and through me. When my goal is not to promote myself, but to promote Him—like John the Baptist, who said "He must increase, but I must decrease" (John 3:30 NASB)—then all my striving, all my stress, and all my busywork fall to the wayside and much peace—and rest—follows.

First Peter 5:6 tells us that when we humble ourselves before God (and admit we can do nothing on our own), He will raise us up in due time. Peter, who wrote that verse, might have been inspired by one of David's songs that says of God, "You stoop down to make me great" (Psalm 18:35). What a goal for us as godly women...to exalt God so highly above ourselves and to maintain a true humility about who we are in comparison to Him. That is truly when He decides to exalt us, isn't it? When He knows we are humble enough that we will not take the glory for ourselves. For when He exalts us, it is for His glory in the first place, so that others around us will see we had nothing to do with our success and will praise God for what He did in our life. That's the way He wants it. That's the way He wants us. Thus, He tells us to leave behind the striving and the stress that accompanies it, and wait on Him.

God's Principle of Promotion

Several years ago my mother-in-law quoted a verse to me over the phone while encouraging me as a young writer. It's become a verse that I often have to recall when I am tempted to strive and stress over the promoting of my work and ministry. The verse was Psalm 75:6: "Promotion cometh neither from the east, nor from the west, nor the south. But God is the judge: he putteth down one, and setteth up another" (KJV). I find it interesting that the verse leaves out the direction of north when it says promotion doesn't come from the east, west, or south. Some Bible teachers say that's because promotion or advancement comes from God above...from the Great White North...when God sees our hearts can handle what He has coming. What better reminder, again, to stop striving and leave the success and the promotions in His hands.

Waiting for God's Best

Early in my writing and speaking career, I had dinner in Dallas with a more seasoned author from my publishing house who appeared to be enjoying much success with her books and her speaking. When I talked with Michelle about my ministry and how I was hoping to be speaking and writing so much more, she leaned in close and said, "Girlfriend, you've got a husband, and a child…if I had that, I would not be doing this at the rate I'm doing it. I do hope one day to have a family, and then I won't be doing this so much.

"You trust God, girl. And you wait for Him to bring you what He wants for you in His perfect timing. Why would you want to strive for and go after what is only gonna be half as good as what God can give you if you just wait?"

I took Michelle's words to heart. On the flight home, I made a list on the left side of a sheet of paper of all the things I worked for. On the right side of the paper, I wrote all the things God had brought my way that I couldn't have possibly arranged. When I was done with the two columns, there was no comparison between the two! The things that God had brought my way were so much more fruitful, so much greater, so much more rewarding than the few measly things I was able to muster up myself. I began to wonder, too, if those things I strove for on the left side of the paper would've been much bigger and better if I had simply waited and let God bring them to me in His own way and time.

My friend's wise words continue to hold true. When I find myself starting to strive, starting to worry about what more I can do to advance my career, I remind myself that God can give me so much more and something so much better if I just remain still and yield to Him. I can strive and tire myself out getting a little bit more of what I think is best, or I can wait on God and be refreshed as He gives me what is far better.

I have since found that my greatest stress reliever these days—my greatest island hideaway in Him—is surrender: kneeling before God and saying "I don't have to have all this…I only want

You and what You have for me." Then I watch Him pour rest and relief into my life as He reminds me there is nothing I have that He hasn't first given me anyway.

Are you beginning to get a glimpse of the kind of rest and peace you can experience when you finally realize it isn't your job to promote or advance or market yourself, but to rest in God and trust that He will promote us in His own way and in His own perfect timing?

Toiling or Trusting?

Just in case you're still wondering how all this resting is going to get you ahead of the game, I want to share with you two real-life situations—on opposite ends of the spectrum—of what happens when we 1) choose to work ourselves silly; or 2) choose to do what we feel is right and trust God to honor us in due time.

"Maria" works long hours at the office while her only daughter is in after-school care until 6:00 or 7:00 P.M. every weekday evening. "I know I won't get fired if I leave the office at 4:30, along with everyone else," she told me one day. "But I think staying later and working harder is expected if I want to prove myself and be seen as doing a good job." Yet she wrestles with the guilt of not being more available to her daughter. "I have to do what I have to do," she rationalizes.

Here is where we must ask: To whom are we trying to prove ourselves? Who is it we are hoping to impress, and who is it we are hoping will say, "Good job"?

"Chelsea" works at an office job, too. Being newly married, she was often anxious to complete her work by 5:00 P.M. so she could leave promptly and get home to cook dinner for her husband. "At times I wondered if it looked like I wasn't as committed. Or maybe it just looked like I was lazy," she told me. A couple of her fellow employees even questioned her once about why she wasn't fearful of losing her job, since she never stayed past 5:00 P.M. During Chelsea's first evaluation, her boss said, "I've noticed you always have your work done and you're always out of here by 5:00 P.M. That shows me you have better time management skills than some of the other employees who are often here until 8:00 or 9:00 P.M. For that, I'm giving you a raise." Chelsea ended up getting not only a raise, but a promotion to management soon afterward!

It's clear that God honored Chelsea's intentions to put her family first and strive to please no one other than God. He honored her by causing her to be recognized, not slighted, when it came to the promotion and the impressions from the company. She learned a valuable lesson early in her life and marriage that when her priorities are right and she is trusting God to see her heart, rather than hoping to impress others through her actions, God will indeed honor her at the proper time.

Maria, however, has yet to get a promotion or anything above a cost-of-living raise. She is simply doing what she feels must be done, according to the world's standard of promotion rather than God's standard.

Who is setting the standard by which *you* live? The world, which says you must keep running in order to get what you want? Or God, who says, "Commit to the LORD whatever you do, and your plans will succeed" (Proverbs 16:3)?

What is *your* goal? To be seen as a woman who is capable of doing much? To gain the recognition and admiration of everyone around you? To be a Superwoman who can bring home the bacon, fry it up in a pan, and never let your husband forget he's your man—in addition to all the other roles and responsibilities you're juggling? That will all take some striving...endless striving. It's all meaningless, chasing after the wind, Ecclesiastes 2:11 says. But if your goal is to be humble and pleasing in the sight of God, if your goal is to exalt Him alone with all that you do, if your goal is to just have Jesus, that will take surrender. And surrender always leads to joy.

The Rewards of Rest

When I cleared my calendar of several events that hectic spring a couple years ago, God abundantly rewarded me in ways I hadn't even imagined. Some old friends of ours came to town unexpectedly and spent the weekend with us (a weekend I would've been gone if I hadn't obediently cleared my calendar). My brother and his new wife, whom I hadn't seen since their wedding a year earlier, also came to town unexpectedly, on the heels of our friends leaving. And I was able to create some lasting memories with my then nine-year-old daughter by taking her to a concert to see one of her favorite Christian music groups.

I have since learned that before committing to something, I need to pray: *Lord, you know where I'll be and what I'll need to be doing, and You already know what blessings await as well, so make it clear to me if I am to work or if I am to rest so I can be fully available to You for service or worship. Don't let me commit to something and lose the reward You might have had for me if I had only rested.*

I now depend on Him to clearly show me if I should work, or rest. And there is such freedom in doing so. Just as God blessed—or "put His hand of favor upon" the day in which He rested (Genesis 2:3; Exodus 20:11), I often see Him putting His hand of favor upon the rest I take as well. He sees it as obedience. He sees it as worship. He sees it as holy. And He often gives me more rest as my reward.

It's Not All Up to You

What a burden was lifted off me the day I really understood it is not up to me to sell a certain number of books per year. It isn't up to me to cause a stirring in women's hearts when I speak. It isn't up to me to ensure that every woman in my church maintains a certain level of spiritual growth. It isn't up to me to change my husband or my daughter. That is all God's work. I must simply be obedient, and humble, and continue to rely on Him to use me as an instrument to do the work that only He can. What a relief that awareness is to what could be an otherwise overwhelming life.

In your life, the same holds true:

- It's not up to you to make all things work together for good in your home, your career, or your personal life (Romans 8:28).

- It's not up to you to "save" your husband, child, or loved one (Ephesians 2:8 THE MESSAGE).

- It's not up to you to try to make a promotion happen (Psalm 75:6; 1 Peter 5:6).

- It's not up to you to ensure that every job in your church gets completed (1 Corinthians 12:14-31).

- It's not solely up to you to provide for your family's needs (Psalm 127:1-2).

It's not all up to you.

"Apart from me you can do nothing," Jesus stated firmly in John 15:5. And He also said, "With God, all things are possible" (Matthew 19:26). Did you catch that? *With God.* Again, it's not up to you alone to do it all. It's God working alongside you, through you, in spite of you.

"Come to me you who are burdened and I will give you rest," Jesus says to your tired soul that has been striving too long.

It's not up to you, Jesus seems to be saying as well.

So…take a deep breath, my friend, and feel that burden roll off your back and onto the ground beneath your feet. Relax your shoulders and lift up your eyes toward heaven. You were designed to live freely and lightly…and to let God do the work that only He can.

$\mathcal{G}$ive It a Rest

In what areas of your life do you find yourself striving but not being able to get ahead?

Pray Philippians 4:6-7 over the situations you listed above. Then commit them to God (Proverbs 16:3). Write out these verses here to help you memorize them and help you remember to keep from striving:

Try the exercise I did after I talked with Michelle. In the left column, list what you've worked hard to get. On the right side, list what God has provided for you in spite of your efforts or lack of efforts.

What I've worked for: What God brought my way:

Now compare the two lists. What do they tell you about toiling versus trusting?

Thou art the Lord who slept upon the pillow,
Thou art the Lord who soothed the furious sea,
What matter beating wind and tossing billow
If only we are in the boat with Thee?
Hold us in quiet through age-long minute
While Thou art silent, the wind is shrill:
Can the boat sink while Thou, dear Lord, art in it?
Can the heart faint that waiteth on Thy will?

AMY CARMICHAEL

FIVE

Taking Quiet Refuge
in God's Word

EVER HAVE ONE OF THOSE DAYS when God messes with your schedule?

I figured it would be a routine flight from Atlanta, Georgia, to Jackson, Mississippi, and I was hoping the one-hour, 20-minute flight would go quickly so I could get dinner and settle in for a conference I was to speak at two days later. But the ordinary flight I hoped for soon turned spectacular as I watched an incredible lightning show from the air. Bolts of fiery orange shot down into and among darkened clouds (which resembled clumps of trees on the ground in the darkness through my plane window). The fast and furious lightning lit up the sky like a strobe light. The accompanying turbulence caused the plane to dip and swing about, which indicated the storm was getting dangerous. After two hours went by and we still hadn't landed, the pilot informed us we'd been in a holding pattern for 40 minutes, waiting for enough visibility to land in Jackson. But we were short on fuel, and he'd lost contact with the control tower because of the storm, so we had to land in nearby Monroe, Louisiana.

The groans I heard on the plane told me Monroe was not a desirable place to land. And by the time we did, I knew why. We were on a deserted runway at an airport that had shut down for the night, and we were also told there were no rental cars on the premises, so we couldn't get off the plane and drive to our destinations. We were stuck. Besides that, we learned upon landing that our plane had hit a bird during the descent and we wouldn't be allowed to get back up in the air until a contract mechanic was summoned to the scene to survey any possible damage to the plane. (At this point, I was wondering what size bird can damage an MD-80 jet!)

So there we sat, on that deserted runway, for nearly two hours until a mechanic—with a flashlight the size of my ballpoint pen—arrived, shone his miniscule light on a section of the plane, and matter-of-factly said, "No bird damage; you're on your way."

But we couldn't go on our way yet. After the pilot resumed contact with the control tower in Jackson and was preparing to take off, he noticed that two smaller planes had parked on either side of ours while we were waiting on the bird damage survey, and the pilots of those planes had gone home for the night. Because it was against FAA regulations for our pilot to board another airline's plane, he and the flight attendants had to tow the smaller plane on our left out of the way. And because there was no tow bar at the Monroe airport, the pilot and flight attendants got out and literally *pushed* the other plane out of the way. (The passengers weren't allowed to leave the plane because there was no security at the airport to re-secure us before getting back on the plane, so we watched from the windows.)

Once we were back in the air with just 20 minutes to go to arrive in Jackson, I knew something else had to be wrong after nearly an hour had gone by. Sure enough, the pilot then informed us that we were in another holding pattern because the plane's hydraulic system had failed and he was waiting for procedures from the ground on how to land the plane without functioning hydraulics. Another hour seemed to go by, and then we were warned that we'd be doing an emergency landing complete with fire engines alongside the runway just in case the failed hydraulics caused any problems. For fear of our plane exploding and lighting any nearby buildings on fire, our pilot rested the plane in the middle of the airstrip, and we were asked to walk back to the terminal. We *did* finally make it to Jackson, Mississippi—*four hours* after our scheduled arrival time.

After deplaning, I got a clue as to why God was messing with our schedule. Our plane lost contact with the tower in Jackson four hours earlier because an F-3 tornado had hit the town and wiped out the power. The control tower's crew and the entire airport had been evacuated. So while we were in a holding pattern in the air, amidst that awesome lightning show, the people in Jackson were evacuating the town. And while we were sitting for two hours on a quiet deserted airstrip in Monroe, the town of Brandon, where I was to speak two days later, was being devastated by the tornado.

The next afternoon I rode through the town and saw the damage caused by the largest tornado to have hit that area in 11 years. I realized then that God had kept my plane in the air long enough for me to not be on the ground in the middle of that storm. And that plane I had to sit in for a frustrating two hours on that quiet, abandoned airstrip in Louisiana was clearly my shelter from the storm that blew apart Brandon, an hour and a half's driving distance away.

I learned that day to not only thank God for the times He interrupts, slows down, or throws delays into my schedule, but for the times He provides for me a refuge in the storm.

Just as that plane became a refuge for me during the tornado that was wreaking havoc on the ground, God's Word has many times become a refuge for me as well…during the storms of life and the whirlwinds of busyness.

A Refuge in the Storm

As I was preparing to write this book, I took a long walk around a lake in my town. I was concerned because I knew my life didn't look like a life of rest, but I desperately wanted it to. I prayed, "Lord, would you transform my life in such a way that I know clearly what it means to rest in You? Make me a woman who truly slows down and lives a life of rest. Show me what it means to rest."

Now, I'm not sure what I was expecting when I asked God to teach me to rest. Perhaps I expected Him to help me slow down so I could smell the flowers, or maybe I was hoping He'd remind me to walk barefoot in the grass, or make me more disciplined so I would say no to more things and live life at a slower, more enjoyable pace. I was even half hoping He'd send me on a trip to Hawaii and give me opportunities for rest and relaxation. But God didn't do any of that.

Instead, on the morning after praying, "Lord, teach me to rest," the storm blew in.

The church our family attends had been struggling through a transition in leadership and my husband was asked to step in and serve as the church's interim senior pastor. Misunderstandings and accusations about various matters began to arise. Good friends of mine began to leave our church. I found myself wondering how all this had happened so quickly. Then I got a phone call from Paul, who always seems to know what to say at times like that.

"Cindi, the storm just blew in," he said.

"Yeah, I know," I responded.

"Cindi, where was Jesus during the storm?" Paul asked. I hesitated for a minute, not knowing where he was going with all of this. But before I could answer, Paul continued: "He was in the boat—sleeping. The disciples were all panicked about the storm, but Jesus was in the bottom of the boat asleep.

"Cindi, that's what we need to do during this storm. We've got to be resting in the bottom of the boat, just like Jesus was. We need to be so secure in Him and what He's allowing that we act as if we've gone to sleep—until it's over."

"Okay," I responded. "Sleep in the storm." But again I wasn't sure what I was supposed to do with that thought. I thanked Paul for calling and hung up the phone and pretty much forgot about that conversation.

Until the next morning.

When I got out of bed, I went into my study, slid down on the floor behind the closed door, and prayed: "God, I don't want to face today. I don't want to hear anything else about what people are thinking, how we're being perceived, and what's going on. I don't want to talk to anyone and have to explain anything. I don't want to be around anything that's going to remind me of what's happening because it's out of my control. God, would You protect me today? Would You just hem me in and around and isolate me, as if I were a boat out on the water, away from all that's happening on shore?"

And then I remembered—the boat!

I was praying that God would isolate me, protect me from anything that would cause me to panic. But what I was really asking God to do was to take me down into the bottom of the boat, where I could rest with Him.

Upon realizing that, I went to Mark chapter 4 in the Bible and re-read the account of Jesus sleeping in the storm. And I was surprised at what I found.

Just prior to the storm, Jesus said to His disciples, "Let us go over to the other side" (verse 35). Then they left the crowd and prepared to go to the other side of the lake, to a place where Jesus wanted to go. While they were crossing the lake, "a furious squall came up" (verse 37).

Now, the disciples had no reason to be afraid. They were going to a place where Jesus wanted to go. And since God-in-the-flesh was right there with them in the boat, there was nothing that would keep them from getting there. Yet they panicked.

I remembered then that I had asked God a couple days earlier to take me to a new place—a place in my life where I lived out the principles of rest. I had asked God to transform me. And to transform me, He had to take me to a place I hadn't been before. To be transformed, we sometimes have to go through the storm. It was as if Jesus, in response to my prayer, were saying, "You want to be changed? You want to learn about rest? Then let's go over to the other side. There will be a storm on the way, but it's part of the learning process. I'm going to teach you what it means to sleep during the storm. Then you will truly know what it means to rest."

It was then that I realized that while I had asked God to teach me to *rest*, instead, God wanted to teach me to *trust*. He wanted me to know that to rest is to trust. And to trust is to rest.

When we delve into God's Word, or reach for it at a time of crisis, a certain quietness and confidence strengthens us in the process.

I love how Jesus, at the height of the storm, told the wind and the waves, "Quiet! Be still!" (verse 39). Yet it was His panicked disciples who needed to hear and heed that rebuke. Although the text says Jesus rebuked the wind and waves, I like to think He said these words out loud so His disciples would get the hint and the wind and waves simply overheard... and obeyed!

Jesus then turned to His scared, frenzied disciples and asked, "Why are you so afraid? Do you still have no faith?" (verse 40). And God's Word spoke to me that morning, too, as if God Himself were saying, "Cindi, why are you so afraid? Do you still have no faith? Trust Me. I am right here in the boat with you. Don't you think I can get you over to the other side?"

God wanted me to know that to rest is to recognize who is in control and live accordingly. Resting means sleeping peacefully in the storm because we know, personally, the One who can still the wind and waves and get us to safely to the other side.

I was able to "rest in the storm" over the next few months because I had found my refuge in the Word of God. And when I asked God to take me down into the bottom of the boat, where

I could be protected, He took me deeper into His Word, where I could sense Him as my refuge and where I could find His true rest.

A Refuge of Refreshment

In Exodus 14:14, the Bible says, "The LORD will fight for you; you need only to be still." In Psalm 57:1 David wrote, "I will take refuge in the shadow of your wings until the disaster has passed." Verse after verse in God's Word reminds us of God's promise of peace and protection, rest and refuge when we are in the storm, when we are feeling overwhelmed, when we need refreshment for our dry, weary soul.

"In quietness and trust is your strength," says Isaiah 30:15. And when we delve into God's Word, or reach for it at a time of crisis, a certain quietness and confidence strengthens us in the process.

I've experienced several occasions on which I was distraught over a problem, until I remembered words of comfort that I had read in the Bible just prior to the situation occurring. By going to God's Word every day, I am not only quieting myself before God so He can minister to my heart, but I am placing myself in the position where He can prepare me ahead of time for what is to come so I won't be overwhelmed. Perhaps that's how God's Word provides not only a refuge for us, but a *preparation* for when the overwhelming times will come...a way to nestle down into the boat for the storm at hand.

How much of your worry would fall by the wayside if you first went to God and His Word each morning to make sense of your life, calm your fears, strengthen your heart, and encourage yourself? Perhaps you're already doing that, and you've discovered this spiritual nourishment is as essential to your day as food and water.

Jesus said He is the Bread of Life and the Living Water. That makes Him an essential part of our daily—not weekly—lives. We must drink of Him just as we drink of water. We must feed on His Word just as we feed on nutritious foods.

Time to Sit Down

So, how can you feed on the Word of God? You can start by sitting down and getting quiet. British missionary Amy Carmichael, known for her tremendous service in India and her great sacrifices so she could follow the will and heart of God, wrote, "Those who do most in the day and who always have time for one thing more are those who know what it is to sit down on the green grass. It is not the bustling, chattery people who do most for others. It is those who know most of quietness." She explained, in her book *Whispers of His Power,* that before Jesus could feed the people, He had them "sit down in groups on the green grass" (Mark 6:39). "Before He can feed us we too must sit down. David sat before the Lord; he was quiet before his God. Even if we have not a long time to spend in the morning with our God, much can be received in a very few minutes if only we are quiet. Sometimes it takes a little while to gather our scattered thoughts and quiet our soul. Even so, don't hurry; make it sit down on the green grass."[1]

If you're having trouble sitting down on the grass so God can feed you, here is a plan to help quiet your heart and get you started.

Start with a song—I have found one excellent way to quiet my heart and prepare myself for God's Word is through worshipful music. Sometimes I will play a song from a worship CD. Other times I will sing one that I know by heart. Still other times, I reach for a hymnal and sing an old song like "Savior, like a Shepherd Lead Us"—a song that brings me back to the simplicity of the relationship: Jesus and me.

There are many songs of thanksgiving and praise in the Bible, and most of them are in the Psalms. So, you could start there as well. Pick a psalm. Because they're so full of human emotion, you will find your heart connected with God's right away in an attitude of praise and humility. Read the psalm aloud. Pick a tune and sing it. Think on it. Pray it through. Journal the psalm and personalize it. Already your heart will be quieted by being in God's presence and taking in His Word.

Sift through the stories—Just as I found comfort in the passage about Jesus sleeping in the storm, you may know of a story in the Bible that would be particularly meaningful to you. If so, turn to it and read it through. If not, start in one of the Gospels (Matthew, Mark, Luke, or John) and just read about Jesus' life and interaction with people until something stops you. Put yourself in the picture. Could He be saying those words to you? How would you respond if you were the one He was addressing? Pray about what God wants you to know through what you've read.

Study the meaning and application—If you're in the place where you're longing for deeper rest and refreshment from God's Word, it's time to go beyond the basics. As your hunger for God's Word grows, study His Word more. Spend time with it. Stay in a certain passage for a week or longer. Chew on it. Meditate on it. Journal your responses to it. Get some commentaries and study some of the original Hebrew or Greek words used in the text. There is no end to what you can discover in God's Word. The key to fruitful study is to ask three questions about every text you read: 1) What does the passage say? 2) What does it mean (in its cultural, literal context)? 3) What does it teach me (for my life and situation)?

Hungering for the Word

On days when I've longed for God's refreshment, I've read through Psalm 119—a long song about the refreshment, encouragement, purity, and righteousness of God's Word. Nothing will instill a hunger and longing for the Word of God more than reading through and meditating on this psalm. It's divided into 22 sections, and in the original Hebrew text, each section is a poetic stanza that begins with the next letter of the Hebrew alphabet. Try reading Psalm 119 in these 22 sections, making these your "daily bread" for the next month, and see how the text increases your appetite for God's Word.

As you're "eating well" and "resting often" in the Word of God, may you be able to say, as the psalmist did, "Oh, how I love your law! I think about it all day long" (Psalm 119:97 NLT). For God's law not only offers refreshment for our tired souls, but a secure refuge in the storm.

Think about it for a few moments. Wouldn't it be nice right now to go down with Him to the bottom of the boat, where you can get some true rest?

Resting in God's Word

TAKE YOUR BIBLE, A PEN, AND THIS BOOK and go someplace where you can be alone for about a half hour. If possible, go to your backyard, a nearby park or lake, or someplace where you can be alone and relish in the beauty of what God has created. (Keep in mind you can use this exercise as a model for a "quiet time in Scripture" with nearly any psalm or passage from the Bible. The possibilities are endless. So sit down in your quiet place and enjoy your refuge—and refreshment—in God's Word.)

Once you find your location, you're ready to begin:

Alone with the Shepherd of Your Heart

- Clear your mind of any personal agendas or distracting thoughts.
- Ask God for an open heart to hear what He wants to say to you.
- Confess any desire to rush through this time.
- Relax and enjoy being in God's presence.

Hear the voice of Jesus speak to your heart:

Welcome to this quiet time with Me, My beloved...how often I've wanted to gather you in My arms and hold you close to My heart. Perhaps now we can talk about how the two of us can become closer.

Turn in My Word to Psalm 23. My servant, David, wrote this about Me. I want you to know Me as your Rest and Refuge in the same way that David knew Me as his Good Shepherd. Read it slowly, thinking of Me as your Provider of Rest, asking Me to show you new truths about My love and gentleness that you have never realized before.

Now that you've read it, I want to talk with you about our relationship. Do you find that you are "in want" about anything? If so, what is it that you desire more than My love?

In what ways can you recall that I have made you lie down in green pastures?

Are you longing for quiet waters in your life? Describe to Me what those quiet waters would look like.

Can you recall times when I have led you beside quiet waters such as those?

In what ways do you need Me to restore your soul?

In what ways do you need My rod to protect you from the wolves? Do you recognize what wolves are in your life right now?

Describe a time when you've sensed My staff around your neck, pulling you back to My side.

If you cannot recall times I have led you, is it because you have not followed? Talk to Me about what's on your heart so we can have this kind of close relationship.

Now, read this psalm again, this time discussing it with Me. I love to hear your thoughts, your concerns, your questions, your fears, your words of praise.

You know, I've written you a whole book about My love for you. Would you write Me just a letter, a prayer, or a song expressing your heart to Me? Go ahead...pour out your heart. And remember, My beloved...your words are safe with Me. I am a refuge for you.

My song, letter, or poem to the Lord:

oise and crowds have a way of siphoning our energy and distracting our attention, making prayer an added chore rather than a comforting relief.

CHARLES R. SWINDOLL

Every time you get into personal contact with Jesus, His words are real. "My peace I give unto you," it is a peace all over from the crown of the head to the sole of the feet, an irrepressible confidence.

OSWALD CHAMBERS

Six

Experiencing Peace and Power Through Prayer

JENNIFER AMAZES ME when it comes to prayer.

When I'm struggling with something I haven't told anyone about, she is the one who will call, out of the blue, and tell me she's praying for me in the same area with which I'm struggling. When my husband, a pastor, announces to the congregation the direction of the church, or what he'll preach on next, it's often no surprise to Jennifer. She'd already been praying to that effect months earlier.

When I experienced a profoundly powerful response from the audience at one particular retreat, I learned upon arriving home that Jennifer was deep in prayer during the same hour that I was speaking. She had prayed for women's hearts to be opened toward the Lord. And the scriptures she was praying for me and the women that morning were the same ones I was speaking on, although she had no idea at the time. The stories are endless; the timing is impeccable. There's no doubt Jennifer's prayer life is powerful.

Jennifer also has a full-time job that can be pretty stressful now and then. But you'd never know it. Jennifer displays more peace and calm and serenity than anyone else I know.

It must have something to do with the fact that she prays.

Prayer slows us down, that's for sure. It takes us out of the driver's seat and puts us in a position where we're ever reminded that God is in control. It brings peace and calm to our lives. So if we truly want a life that is restful, we must become women who pray.

But how do we find the time?

Too Busy to Pray

In his popular book *Too Busy Not to Pray*, pastor Bill Hybels wrote: "To people in the fast lane, determined to make it on their own, prayer is an embarrassing interruption."[1] Later he said, "Prayerless people cut themselves off from God's prevailing power, and the frequent result is the familiar feeling of being overwhelmed, overrun, beaten down, pushed around, defeated."[2] Have you ever considered that you could be feeling overwhelmed, overrun, beaten down, pushed around, and defeated simply because you aren't taking the time to pray?

I remember one of the most defeating weeks I'd had in a long time. Looking back, it was a week in which I was too busy to pray.

I was just a couple months into leading the women's ministry at my church and I was feeling overwhelmed at all there was to do. At the same time, a book I'd written had just been released, I was preparing to speak at a couple of conferences, and I had to go on a major trip planned by my publisher. Life was exciting. I was living my dream. But God gently knocked on the door of my heart one day as if to say, "Do you remember Me? Do you remember who got you here? Do you even know what it means to commune with Me anymore?"

This defeating week was the week before our new women's Bible studies were to start for the year, and I was following up and seeing if all the leaders were ready, encouraging them, making sure they had their materials and all the promotional letters were sent out. At the same time, I was doing a lot of other work and trying to run my own writing and speaking ministry.

And then the first arrow was launched.

On Sunday, two days before one of our studies was to start, one of my leaders came to me with a crisis in her marriage. She was fresh into ministry and excited to be leading a small group for praying wives. But she'd just discovered her husband was having an affair. "I don't think I can do this," she told me. We talked and cried and prayed. And I thought, *Why now, God? Of all people, why her?*

The following morning, on Monday, I called Annie, the woman who had just agreed to take over the prayer responsibilities for our women's ministry. But I couldn't get ahold of her. I remember thinking, *Why now, God? I need her to be praying!*

The next day, Tuesday, only three women showed up on the opening night of a Bible study in which we expected about 10 to 15 women. And I thought, *Why now, God? Just when I take over the women's ministry, the attendance at the Bible studies is going way down!*

The following night—Wednesday—was the opening night of another study that had been very popular the preceding fall... and not a woman showed up, except the leader and the woman at whose house the study was held. Exasperated, I thought, *What's next?*

Then on Thursday morning, I got a call from a woman on my women's ministry leadership team telling me that Victoria, one of our study leaders, was in the hospital. As I drove to see her, I thought, *Why her, Lord? She's been through so much already!*

I visited with Victoria in the hospital that afternoon and prayed with her. As I was leaving the room, she made a comment that opened my eyes to what had been happening and gave me the answer to all my "Why Lord?" questions that week. She said, "Would you give a message to the other women who are teaching the praying wives study on Tuesday? I promised them we'd get together and pray before their study was to start. I told them wild horses wouldn't keep me from praying with them—but we were never able to get together because I ended up here. Would you tell them I've been praying for them anyway, right here in this hospital bed?"

Then I realized what was happening. I finally got it.

Victoria had committed herself to praying with those women, but she had been sidelined so it wouldn't happen. The one thing all those women under attack that week had in common was that they were on the front lines of the battle, prepared to start those Bible studies that would make a difference in women's lives. They were also the prayer power in the women's ministry in our church, and the enemy was taking them out one by one. What's more, each of these women had been poised on the front lines of battle and their commander (that would be me) was too busy "doing ministry" to really pray for them. I was too distracted by busyness to pray for their protection and the strength they would need against the arrows that would inevitably be launched at them.

As I drove home from the hospital, I realized the question that God wanted me to ask all along was not "Why, Lord?" but "Why not *me*, Lord?" I was their leader, but why wasn't I sidelined? Why wasn't I facing the attacks? And the answer shot through me clear as a bell: *You were not a threat! You were too busy to pray!*

I felt an awful knot in my stomach and conviction shot through me. I was not standing in the gap for those women who were being taken out one by one. In fact, Annie, who was not available when I called her on Monday to pray, was the one carrying most of the load, and she was in a hospital bed with an intense fever and pain, all the while praying intensely for our women. But I had been too busy that week, too wrapped up in my own life to petition God about greater purposes.

When I called Annie from my car on the drive home and discovered all she had gone through that week as she stood in the prayer gap alone for our women, I apologized and, in tears, I asked her what I could do to make sure it never happened again.

Annie said, "It only takes one time to feel that sinking feeling of regret—*if only I'd prayed*—to make you a person who prioritizes prayer."

Annie was right. That's all it took for me to allow God to rearrange my life so I would be a person of prayer. As I finished my drive home that day, I prayed. For the first time in a long time, I *really* prayed: "God, I'm so sorry. I never again want to be so busy that I fail to pray. If the powers of darkness don't consider me a threat because of a pathetic prayer life, then I'm of no use to You at all. So please do what it takes in my life to bring me to my knees in prayer."

God did just that. He began to open my eyes and convict my heart with the fact that He does not care how many books I write, how many times a year I speak, or how popular our women's ministry is in the local community. He cares, rather, how well I am shepherding the women under my care, how long I am willing to stand in the gap for them in prayer, how long I'm sitting at His feet for direction on how to lead them.

I now know better than to let myself get even close to being too busy to pray.

And I still don't get it right sometimes. There are days when the unexpected rolls in and I find myself again on the fly, feeling regret that I didn't take adequate time earlier that day for prayer. But for the most part, God has convicted my heart so heavily that I now know better than to let myself get even close to being too busy to pray.

Trying to Squeeze It In

I know I'm not the only one who's had seasons of life when I've neglected prayer...and paid the consequences for it. Shortly after my experience, I read an article entitled "Too Busy to Pray?" in a Christian magazine. But rather than being convicted all over again, instead, I was frustrated at the way the article implied that all of us are busy and so we should take advantage of creative ways to *slip in* conversations with God amidst the hectic pace of our lives. The article's suggestions for how to "pray more without changing your schedule" included praying while on hold on the phone and "muting the television during commercial breaks to pray." I remember thinking that if my prayer life ever came down to squeezing it in while I'm put on hold or during television commercial breaks, I was in deep trouble. After all, communion with the almighty God is an experience to look forward to, an occasion to plan for and enjoy—not something to slip in dutifully between our moments of entertainment or work. Prayer is a privilege we should make the most of. It is a necessity that takes time, not merely a luxury or an afterthought. Lord help us if we ever run so fast that we can only pray "on the fly."

Why Take the Time to Pray?

Besides the fact that God longs for our communion with Him, there are some practical reasons to pray if we are women who are longing for rest. Prayer has a way of making our otherwise overwhelming lives much more manageable and enjoyable.

• **Prayer unleashes *power* into our lives**

Prayer not only evokes the power of God into situations we're praying for, but it brings a fresh wind and fire into our lives as we pray. And that fresh wind of power is often needed to enable us to get our work done. Charles Spurgeon once quoted Martin Luther as saying, "I have so much to do today that I shall never get through it with less than three hours' prayer."[3] I can relate... not to three hours of prayer every morning, but to not getting anything done if I don't designate significant time to pray each day. Unlike Martin Luther, we tend to think, however, that we have too much to do, and therefore no time left to pray. Thus we give in to a life that is even more overwhelming. As Hybels says, "Surprising numbers of people are willing to settle for lives like that. Don't be one of them. Nobody has to live like that. Prayer is the key to unlocking God's prevailing power in your life."[4]

• Prayer ushers *peace* into our lives

When David the psalmist was overwhelmed, he found peace in laying all his concerns before God in prayer: "I pour out my complaints before him and tell him all my troubles. For I am over-whelmed" (Psalm 142:2-3 NLT). In Philippians 4:6-7 we're told, "Don't worry about anything; instead, pray about everything. Tell God what you need, and thank him for all he has done. If you do this, you will experience God's peace, which is far more wonderful than the human mind can understand. His peace will guard your hearts and minds as you live in Christ Jesus" (NLT).

When Jesus told us to come to Him with our burdens and He will give us rest (Matthew 11:28-29), He was saying, "Lay it all down. Give it to Me in prayer. I will take the burden and give you peace in its place." Now that's quite an exchange—our bur-dens for His peace.

There is something not only peaceful but relaxing about prayer. Have you ever considered that might explain why we tend to fall asleep so easily at night while we're praying? Prayer does something to slow us down, still our souls, and cause us to relax in God's arms. I don't feel guilty for falling asleep during prayer, because what better way to enter our unconscious state than when our last waking thoughts were spent in communion with Him? Falling asleep while we're praying at night has to be the closest thing to falling asleep in God's arms.

• Prayer unfolds *perspective* into our lives

When we pray, we are acknowledging that God is in control and we are not. We are practicing our dependence on Him. We are clarifying, to us and to Him, that we understand the order: He is God above, and we are here below. That is a good reminder for us to not run around harried, trying to accomplish everything. It's also a good way to relieve from our minds the pressures we so often feel we must carry ourselves.

Many times when I pray, God changes my mind about things, or reinforces the importance of certain things, or gives me the insight needed to see things in a new light.

A friend of mine recently experienced this during a time of small-group prayer at church. He was trying to keep his four-year-old son, Gabriel, quiet so he could pray with the other adults. But his son wanted daddy's attention so he could talk about other things. My friend says, "I actually had a stoplight experience during our prayer time. I looked at Gabe while we were praying and thought about how fast he is growing up. I also saw me in him. Here he is talking to his dad, and I am trying to keep him quiet—much like when I approach our Father in heaven. I'm like Gabe, easily distracted, wanting to talk about things I am interested in, rather than listening to the Lord, who is trying to quiet me down and get me to pay attention to Him."

What does God want to teach or show you in your quiet time with Him? Listening to God is a big part of praying. In fact, during the times when we do less talking, we can hear from Him and His perspective can become ours.

Ways to Pray

If you're struggling with finding the time or knowing what to do during your prayer time, here are some easy ways to get started:

1. *Write out your prayers*—Starting each day with a few minutes of reflective writing can do wonders for the soul and your relationship with God. *But I'm not a writer,* you may be thinking. That's okay. You're a pray-er—at least, you are now! Write to God the same way you'd write a letter to someone you love. Start with praise: "I love you, God. You are the reason I'm alive today. I want to remember that in all I do...." If you need help, go to the book of

Psalms. Those are songs written from the heart to God. Copy the format or the style, or develop your own.

2. *Reflect on yesterday*—A good way to get your life in perspective and turn it over to God is to write about the previous day. By reflecting on yesterday, you'll learn from your mistakes and grow. I know some people who brag about running so fast they never have a chance to look back. They must think that's biblical. After all, Philippians 3:13 tells us to forget what lies behind and strain toward what lies ahead and press on in our work for the kingdom. But that biblical admonishment means we're not to become complacent or stagnant in our spiritual progress. It's not telling us to never look back to learn from our mistakes. Otherwise, how can we possibly grow and mature? Shouldn't we stop long enough to evaluate whether or not we did the right thing? And where does repentance come in? If we're running so fast that we never look back, it's very possible we're offending God and others we've run over in our race, and as a result, we'll fail to take time to make things right. Adjust your pace so you can stop long enough to reflect. And you'll grow in the process.

3. *Keep a prayer journal of who and what to pray for*—You may find yourself overwhelmed at the thought of where to start. So many things to pray for, so little time. I often find myself thinking that. My husband prays for certain people and certain situations on certain days of the week. I've found this helpful, too. Rather than praying about everything every day, and feeling stressed over what you're missing, try making Monday the day you pray for your spiritual growth, as well as that of your husband's and children's. Perhaps Tuesday is the day you can pray for your church and pastor, and for those whom God lays on your heart. Wednesday might be the day for wholehearted

listening, when you ask God to lay on your heart what He wants you to pray about. Try not to "box in" your prayer life, but have an idea of where to start and then let the Spirit lead and prompt you in the direction you ought to pray.

Make Prayer a Throne-Room Experience

A friend of mine said when she was a newer Christian, she was somewhat intimidated by the thought of entering the throne room of the Lord, where she could sit right before Him and share from the deepest parts of her heart.

"I pictured myself at the bottom of a flight of stairs staring up at God, hoping to be heard," she said. "So I began to start each prayer with, 'Jesus I want to be like the women at your feet—washing Your feet with my tears, breaking my alabaster jar of oil, kneeling before You at the cross, there rejoicing at the empty tomb.'

"As I pictured my life's events—my prayers—as if I were one of these women, I was able to see the King's throne in a different light. Not as the throne of an unapproachable ruler—a seat with a high back and ornate armrests—but instead as a beautiful, majestic comfortable couch where I could climb up anytime I wanted to. There would always be room for me because my Father is the King."

God's throne room became a place where she wanted to go often and remain for awhile. Heartfelt prayer does that to us. It ushers us into God's throne room, where He welcomes us with open arms and we feel more of a longing to stay.

Lighten Your Load

One of the most wonderful benefits I've received from frequent prayer in my life has been the way God uses it to shift my focus to what He wants me to do, rather than all the things I think I must do. When I come to Him with a mind and heart that is overwhelmed by all that I feel must be done, and all that must be prayed about, I am comforted as the load lightens, and I come to realize I do not have to change everything, do everything, or make it all happen. Rather, I need only to—as an old hymn says—"take it to the Lord in prayer."[5]

Ruth Myers, in her book *The Perfect Love*, recorded a beautiful prayer for women who often feel overwhelmed and loaded down with life's responsibilities. I'm including it here to help *you* lighten your load by leaving it at Jesus' feet:

Dear Lord,
I quietly leave in Your hand
each concern that could cause me stress today:
    The things You want me to do
        and the things You want me to leave unfinished or even unstarted.
    The relationships You want me to have
        and the ones You want to withhold or take away.
    The joys You will bring my way,
        and the trials you will allow or send.
    The ways You want me to succeed
        and the ways You may let me fail, or seem to fail.
    The opportunities You want me to accept
        and the ones You want me to pass up.
    The doors You want to open
        and the ones You want to close.
    The ways I would like to glorify You
        and the ways You may use others instead of me.
    The times You want me to meet people's needs actively,
        and the times You want me just to listen,
        or to stand aside and "merely" pray.
    The deadlines You want me to meet
        and the ones You may want me to miss.
    The results of my labors—
        great or small, noticed or hidden.
    The ways I will bless or disappoint other people,
        and the ways they will bless or disappoint me.

The human approvals that You will give,
    and the disapprovals that will prod me to rest
    in Your gracious evaluation.
I leave it all quietly to You, my God,
and depend on You to work in me and in those I love:
    to nurture and protect
    to tear down and to build up
    to wound and to heal
    to reprove and to guide—
    as it seems best to You, my wise and loving Father.
I step out of Your shoes and leave Your responsibilities to You.
I let my life drop back behind You, to follow at the pace You prescribe.
Help me sense inner tensions quickly and then "leave it all quietly
    to You."
I am Your servant. I'm available to You to fulfill Your purposes,
    and Yours alone, in Your way and time.
Amen.[6]

Could that be *your* prayer today? When you slow down long
enough to pour your heart out to Him, you'll experience His
peace—and power—like never before.

Experiencing the Power

TRY WRITING OUT A PRAYER similar to that at the close of this chapter. You may want to go line by line and then express your own thoughts and words here. In doing this, you are performing an act of surrender that brings peace—and God's power—into your life.

Whenever peace does not come, tarry til it does or find out the reason why it does not.

OSWALD CHAMBERS

SEVEN

Refreshing Your Heart Through Worship

OVERWHELMED BY THE PILE OF PAPERS on my desk and the drove of dishes in my sink, I grudgingly turned on the water and prepared to hand-wash yet *another* load of dirty dishes.

"Lord, why on earth can't I have a stinkin' dishwasher?" I prayed aloud as I squirted dish soap into the rising sink water. "Is that too much to ask for in the twenty-first century?"

There were other things I could be doing instead of standing at the sink washing dishes, I reasoned. I could be in my study writing an article, completing a Bible study, or discipling my neighbor. But no! The dishes had to be washed because without a dishwasher, there was no place to hide them!

As I reached into the soapy water and pulled out a glass, swirled the sponge around in the glass, and then rinsed it clean, I eventually did what I couldn't help but do next: I sang.

In the midst of the repetition of a boring and meaningless task, I sang to the Lord. I sang hymns I learned in Sunday school as a child. I sang upbeat songs I learned at high school camp. I sang songs of worship to my King. And it wasn't long before my bitterness at not having a dishwasher dissolved into joy at simply having life and breath to sing.

Lifting your voice when you're loaded down with pressure or responsibilities changes you. Praising the Lord, in spite of your problems, transforms you. And singing in the struggles—or simply the stresses—of life helps give you a whole new focus that can change your perspective.

As women who long for rest, we must be women who worship. There is no more direct route from stress to peace, and no better way to transform otherwise mundane work into service done out of love for the Lord.

Today I have a dishwasher in my new home. But there are times when I miss the way the Lord would box me in at that little sink at my old house and force me to offer Him the sacrifice of praise. Those became precious moments between my Maker and me. That's why, once in a while, I'll skip the pots and pans cycle on the dishwasher, fill up my new sink with soapy water, and hand-wash the cookware…so I can relive those simpler days when God delighted in my heartfelt praise.

Why Worship?

Worship slows us down and ushers us into the throne room of the almighty God. It places us in a position where He can reveal Himself to us, which simply causes us to worship Him all the more. It adds meaning to our life. And it gives us a sense of fulfillment and peace.

We were created for God's pleasure. And God takes pleasure when we worship Him by living in the awareness of His presence and proclaiming His goodness in our lives. Worship is a natural expression of our relationship with the living God. It's the way we show Him we love Him. It's the way we stay in a place where God wants us. It's the way we slow down and live differently. And it's imperative if we are to become women who experience rest.

It's been said of legendary Christian music artist Rich Mullins—who is credited with shaping much of today's worship songs and culture—that he was able to take the mundane and turn it into the majestic.

That is something every person, created in the image of God, has the potential to do—take the mundane and make it majestic. You can take your pile of dirty dishes and turn it into an opportunity for praise. Clean your messy desk and make it a time of thanking God for the work He has given you. Drive the long commute and turn it into a concert of praise as you sing to Him on the freeway.

We must learn to live in such a way that worship flows from our hearts, slows us down, and causes us to rest.

Worship refreshes our hearts and makes us come alive. It is what we were made for and therefore it drives us toward our purpose. But if we're too busy to worship, then in a sense we're too busy to live. And so we must learn to live in such a way that worship flows from our hearts, slows us down, and causes us to rest.

In his devotional book *Worship*, singer and songwriter Michael W. Smith says, "When His people cry out to Him with pure hearts, when they sing joyfully about His goodness and grace, when they sit quietly and wait to hear from Him in the midst of their busy day, God shows up. And why wouldn't He? Like all fathers, He delights in spending time with His children."[1]

God calls us to praise Him. He actually looks forward to the times we will meet Him and indulge Him with our praise. When I go for long periods of time during which I haven't been alone with God or pondered on His majesty, I get restless and convicted, like a part of me is out of sync. That's because it is. Because I was made to worship. To express worship, to sing in worship, to live worship. Just as our cars need regular oil changes and tune-ups to keep them running effectively, and just as our bodies need food, water, exercise, and sleep to function properly, you and I need to regularly reconnect with our Maker, through worship, to live the kind of lives God meant us to live (and to outlive the wear and tear busyness causes on our lives).

We looked in chapter 6 at how prayer gets us focused and brings peace and power into our lives. While prayer focuses us, praise turns our hearts around. A song slows us down. Lifting our hands lifts our perspective. And as a result, we become refreshed.

What's Your Worship Style?

I start my day in worship by sitting on the floor up against my closed study door. I am reminded, down on the floor, where I came from, and who I am apart from Christ. Being on the floor puts me in perspective…it's a physical reminder that I am down here, God is up there, exalted on the throne, and it is by His grace, His coming down to me, that I can meet with Him each day.

Also, as I look around the room, I am reminded of all He has given me. The pictures of my family that line my desk remind me of the blessings He has given me in that each of my family members knows God through a personal relationship with Christ. The awards on the wall bear evidence of His grace and the times He decided to promote me. The books I have written, or contributed to, that line my shelves are symbols of what He has done through me. What do I have that hasn't been given to me?[2] What can I give to Him that He has not given me first? All that I am is because of Him, so I want all that I am to return to Him in worship and praise.

Becky, a 21-year-old lover of God and nursing major who is looking to serve the Lord in missions, says she regains her sense of rest and worship by singing whatever praise and worship songs come to her mind.

"I also dance for the Lord in worship. I love to dance; it places some fun back in my life. And when I dance for the Lord, it brings a smile to my face, because I know He is smiling at me," Becky says.

King David danced before the Lord when he was overcome with joy and praise at all God had done for His people. Miriam, the sister of Moses, picked up a tambourine and sang and danced before the Lord when she was overwhelmed with joy at His protection of His people by bringing them through the Red Sea on dry land.

My friend, Carrie, is a worship leader and songwriter. She regains her sense of rest and worship by sipping coffee at a nearby lake, reading, knitting, or crocheting. Those things slow her down and cause her to focus on—and worship—her Creator.

"Resting and worshiping always deepen my relationship with God," Carrie says. "We were created to listen for and to His precious voice. Life is infinitely more worthwhile and fulfilling when I live according to His purposes for my life."

Ways to Worship

How can you make worship a part of your everyday life? By asking God to slow you down and open your eyes every day to see Him in the ways He wants to reveal Himself. Then you can't help but respond in worship.

"The revelation of God is the fuel for the fire of our worship," says Matt Redman in *The Unquenchable Worshipper*. "And there is always more fuel for the fire. When we open the eyes of our hearts, God's revelation comes flying at us from so many different angles. He has revealed Himself to us in creation, through the history of His people and overwhelmingly at the Cross. And to this day every breath we breathe is a reminder of our maker, and every hour holds the possibility of living in His presence."[3]

Worship can flow from us like living water when God reveals Himself to us. But how can it flow from you like living water that refreshes your soul and revives your tired body? It starts by drawing from a number of wells.

Draw from the Well of Experience—In Psalm 32:7 David said to God, "You are my hiding place! You protect me from trouble, and you put songs in my heart because you have saved me" (CEV). I love that—God puts songs in our hearts! We cannot help but worship God when He does something extraordinary in our life. When He parted the Red Sea, the people sang. When He saved David from his enemies, David sang. When the disciples broke bread with Jesus in the upper room, they sang. When you and I take time from our busy day to reflect on what He did for us at Calvary, we can't help but sing…and be refreshed in the process.

Draw from the Well of His Word—Psalm 119:54 says, "No matter where I am, your teachings fill me with songs" (CEV). Look at that verse in other translations:

- "Your decrees are the theme of my song wherever I lodge" (NIV).

- "Your principles have been the music of my life throughout the years of my pilgrimage" (NLT).

- "I set your instructions to music and sing them as I walk this pilgrim way" (THE MESSAGE).

God's Word has been the source of inspiration for many hymns and spiritual songs. It is also the inspiration behind many books, poems, paintings, and plays. When we get into God's Word, we can't help but praise Him for who He is. Reading Psalm 145 aloud (and Psalms 146–150, for that matter!) is another way of worshiping Him. My friend, Nicky, says she finds rest, peace, and solace in worshiping God by reading through her Bible, aloud, while she's in the bathtub. "Reading out loud has helped me tremendously (in retaining God's Word *and* gaining a sense of relaxation and relief) and gives me rest as I discover and remember His Word."

Draw from the Well of What He's Created—One of my friends makes a practice of what she calls "finding my perfect moment." She has trained herself to search out just a moment or two—every day—in which she feels the sun on her back or a warm breeze on her face or hears a chirping bird or the sound of a flowing river. She then closes her eyes and whispers a prayer of gratitude to God for what He just gave her. This not only teaches her to search for quietness and beauty, but calms her heart in the midst of hectic activity and centers her in a position of praise.

Another friend practices praise each time she sees a rose, a rainbow, a sunset, or a starry night. As we look for signs of beauty or little moments of quietness, we are not only training our minds and bodies to slow down, but we are also teaching our hearts to return to our Creator and say, "Help me notice what You made for me to enjoy, and help me remember that You made me to enjoy You as well."

As you begin looking for just one perfect moment in your day, you may be surprised to soon discover many throughout the day! And don't look only for those perfect moments, but look also for ways to turn ordinary, everyday things into something that's cause for praise. By doing that, you are turning the mundane into the majestic!

Worship Wherever You Go

Worship doesn't have to happen only when no one's looking. And it doesn't have to involve music at all. And it certainly shouldn't be relegated to just a half hour before the sermon on Sundays! Worship ought to be a way of life.

"Praise is not to be a fringe activity in our lives," says author Ruth Meyers, "but a basic occupation. It is essential, not optional. It is to be consistent, not occasional."[4]

Here are some suggestions for making worship more a part of your life, especially during the times you might otherwise feel stressed. (In fact, a good way to remember to worship, rather than worry, is to say to yourself, "Instead of feeling stressed, I choose to feel blessed.") Here are ways to practice that perspective and make worship a part of your everyday life:

- Play worship CDs on your way to work, anytime you're in your car alone, or while you're in the kitchen, and sing along with them. Realize that God is your audience and you're singing for and to Him.

- Go for a walk during your lunch hour and do nothing but thank God for all you see as you walk.

- Go ahead, try it. Fill your sink with soapy water and wash dishes and sing. I'm telling you, it works! (And if you have a dishwasher, why not skip using it every now and then and go out of your way to worship as you do the dishes by hand?)

- Sing a hymn or praise song as you gently rock your child or grandchild to sleep.

- Take your Bible with you and read Scripture aloud in the bathtub (or some other secluded place).

- Write a poem to God (maybe even a simple two-liner) and memorize it.

- Memorize a favorite Scripture verse (yes, this is a form of worship).

- Make it a point to find three reasons to praise God every time you're in a situation in which you want to complain.

Now Is the Time to Worship

Are you starting to get the picture? Worship is opening your eyes to recognize God's worth wherever you are and in the midst of whatever you are doing. It is stepping away from the world and your busy routine long enough to gain a God-perspective and then returning to that routine a changed person. It is a combining of who you are in God and where you are in this world. When the two come together in praise, you'll be offering worship to God. And when you truly worship, your heart will be refreshed.

Come, my friend. *Now* is the time to worship.

Worship as a Way of Life

IN 1 THESSALONIANS 5:18, we are told, "Give thanks in all circumstances, for this is God's will for you in Christ Jesus." List some of the mundane tasks you must complete—at work or at home—and then record some ways you can turn your work into worship:

My "work":   *How I can "worship" in it:*

Borrow or buy a worship CD and listen to a song—and try singing along with it—every morning. Watch how much smoother your day goes by when you put worship first and work second.

Read the following accounts of worship by women in the Bible:

- Miriam's spontaneous and public show of worship (Exodus 15:20-21)

- Hannah's personal song of praise after answered prayer (1 Samuel 2:1-11)

- Mary of Bethany's display of extravagant worship (John 12:1-8)

With which woman can you most relate, and why?

Which woman's picture of praise inspires you to worship in a new way? Why?

In contemporary society our Adversary majors in three things: noise, hurry, and crowds....the seeking out of solitary places was a regular practice for Jesus. So it should be for us.

RICHARD FOSTER

EIGHT

Reviving Yourself in a Spacious Place

IT HAD BEEN AN EXHAUSTING FOUR DAYS and I was relieved to be boarding a plane for home. Having been in three states and another country over the past few days on a tour to promote my book, and having experienced wind, rain, snow, and freezing weather, I was anxious to get back to San Diego by noon that day—back to my family, back to a saner life, and back in the sun! But after a mechanical failure on my plane in Pittsburgh, followed by a computer failure, I missed my connecting flight home out of Chicago. And to my horror, O'Hare Airport—and *all* the outgoing planes, for that matter—was packed on account of spring break. There were no seats available on any planes. There was no way for me to get home.

By this time I was frustrated, to say the least. There was a line of about 30 people in front of me, waiting to get to the customer service desk and receive the disappointing news that they couldn't get home that afternoon, either. I was tired from having run to my connecting flight and found it gone. I was sweating from being bound up in a jacket from the freezing weather outside. And I was nearly in tears at the thought of how disappointed my daughter would be when she discovered I wouldn't be able to pick her up from school that afternoon as I had promised.

God, I just want to get home, I prayed silently while standing in the endless line. Aches and pains that I hadn't felt an hour earlier plagued my body. I wished I'd worn my sneakers. I wished I could just let down and cry. Then, after what seemed like hours, "Fran" broke into my confusion and disappointment from behind the customer service counter.

"How can I help you, ma'am?" Fran asked apologetically. I could tell she really did feel sorry for the passengers who couldn't get where they needed to be. And a bit frazzled. Her concern made me feel bad for *her.*

"Fran," I said as I approached the counter and dropped my bags onto the floor. "I *have* to get home this afternoon. I've been gone for four days and I *promised* my nine-year-old daughter I'd pick her up from school today. Can you *please* find a way—*any* way—to get me to San Diego by two o'clock?"

I could tell Fran didn't like having to handle this one. She frowned and began typing quickly on her computer. "There are no seats available going into San Diego before ten o'clock tonight," she said. I moaned at the thought of spending another 12 hours in the crowded airport and not getting home until well past midnight.

I took a deep breath, remembering that God was in control of my schedule. This wasn't taking Him by surprise, and there was something He wanted me to learn in all of this. "Lord," I prayed silently as Fran shook her head and continued to type on the computer. "Do what You want with me...I asked You to teach me about rest...maybe You want me to rest in You and *Your* solution right now. You're obviously not going to use *mine.*"

Fran looked around, fiddled with her computer some more, and then finally leaned over the counter and whispered, "I'm really not supposed to do this, but if I bump you up to first class, you can take a flight out of here to Denver in a few minutes and then connect to a flight to San Diego out of Denver. You won't get home in time to pick up your daughter from school, but you *will* be there in time to have dinner with her."

Hallelujah! Fran, and the Lord, came through!

Rejoicing as I picked up my bags, I thanked Fran profusely and headed to the gate for the plane going to Denver.

"Lord, it isn't what I had hoped, and it will get me home later than I thought, but it's better than staying here all night," I prayed as I walked toward the plane. "And I will rest in the fact that You are still in control and You know what it is You want me to learn by being on this other plane."

When I finally boarded the plane—my "detour" to San Diego through Denver—I sat in a large, leather seat in first class. For the first time ever on a plane, I had leg room like I never knew it. The person "next" to me was practically a row away. The flight attendant called me "Mrs. McMenamin" (she even pronounced my name right!), and took my coat and hung it on a hook behind my seat. She handed me a glass (not a plastic cup!) of something cool to drink before the rest of the passengers had even boarded the plane. Then she brought me a hot meal (in contrast to the peanuts and soda I've usually gotten!). I sat there looking around, not quite knowing what to do with all that room and all that food and all that special treatment.

Suddenly it dawned on me. I was in a *spacious* place. I was in a place of rest, of first-class treatment. At that moment, I *knew* what God wanted to teach me in that detour. My frantic run through the terminal, the missed plane, the frustrating wait in the customer service line, and the disappointment at being delayed all seemed to fade away into the peace I was experiencing now as I was heading home in style.

It was at that moment that Psalm 18:19, a verse I'd been reflecting on earlier, came to mind:

> He brought me out into a spacious place;
> he rescued me because he delighted in me.

I sat there in that nice leather chair with my steak dinner and glass of Dr. Pepper in front of me, and started to cry. "Lord, You didn't *have* to get me home tonight at all, but You *did*, and You put me in first class to do it. You brought me out into a spacious place for no other reason but that You love me and You saw how frustrated I was at being hemmed in."

Before I prayed those words, God knew all that had been stirring in my heart over the past several days. He saw the frustration I had felt as I left five days earlier for that book tour, knowing I needed to slow down and reprioritize my life (remember that story from chapter 1?). He heard the prayers I had prayed at that retreat before I left: "Show me the resting place. Do what it takes in my life to slow me down and get me back to Your feet." And now, on my trip home, He was showing me that He, in fact, *could* bring me out into a spacious place if I was really ready to leave the rat race; He really could bring rest and refreshment to my life in the most unexpected ways if I would just surrender to Him and trust Him.

Now, I realize God brought me into a spacious place in a very dramatic way. He doesn't always bump us up to first class when we cry out for help. But I believe He wanted me to see and experience, in that instance, the sharp contrast between the crowded airport (like the stressful life I was living back home) and the spacious first-class seat on the trip home (the sane life of rest and peace that I could live from that point on).

Out in the Open

Psalm 18:19 in *The Message* reads,

> He stood me up on a wide-open field;
> I stood there saved—surprised to be loved!

When we are hemmed in and around, crowded by the schedules and the stresses and the stuff in our lives, we can hardly feel loved. Rather, we tend to feel worn out and used up. But when we surrender control of our lives and say, "Teach me what You want, Lord; take me where You want to go and show me what it means to rest in You," He surprises us by taking us to a "spacious place" where we can stretch out, breathe again, and feel His love for us in the "wide-open field." God's Word tells us, "Obsession with self...is a dead end; attention to God leads us out into the open, into a spacious, free life."[1]

Doesn't that sound appealing? Living a spacious, free life? Not one that feels hemmed in with obligations and overwork. Our souls need a spacious place to enjoy God and life. Spacious places allow us to reconnect with God, and we need to be wary of "space stealers" that sneak into our lives and rob us of the opportunities to build the kind of relationship with God that leads to rest.

Identifying Space Stealers

Before we talk about how to find a spacious place, we must first know what it is *not*. These are some of the "space stealers" that make me feel hemmed in, add pressure to my life, or distract me from spending quality time with God. Perhaps they keep you from a spacious place, as well:

Having to Have Something—Now

We live in a society that constantly indulges...instant gratification is the norm, or at least the preferred. I've noticed how this is a characteristic of babies and young children. When they want something, they expect it right then. And when they don't get it? Stress! But a sign of maturity is being able to wait, or being able to go without altogether. When I'm being pressured—by the world or by my own selfish desires—to have something *now*, I've found it freeing to be able to walk away from it entirely and say, "I don't need this right now...and I probably don't need it at all."

Work That Presses In on Me

There's nothing that closes us in more than the tyranny of the urgent. Deadlines, whether self-imposed or put upon us by others, can make us feel cornered. But the fact is, there's *always* more work to do. And regardless of what we might think, the work often can wait. But God's Word often doesn't. Henry Blackaby, author of *Experiencing God*, emphasizes that there are sometimes moments when God is speaking to us, and those are the moments He wants us to act. If we are constantly preoccupied and rushed by work deadlines, we may miss those moments altogether and never get them back again. Don't let a pile of work trick you into thinking it's more important than what God might be trying to say to you at a given moment.

Drivenness

I tend to be an overachiever. If I don't put limits on myself or ask God to constantly remind me that I don't have to do it all, I could easily continue to strive. But I want to heed God's call, "Cease striving and know that I am God."[2] Why am I trying to do so much? To impress others? To prove to myself I can do it? Again, God is not impressed with how fast I can run and how much I can accomplish, but rather with how long I am willing to sit at His feet and learn of Him. So I must continually be on the alert for a sense of drivenness that sneaks up and gets me running into a crowded place, rather than waiting on God in a spacious place.

Because our souls need that spacious place where we can enjoy God and life, we must know how to get there—and stay there.

Waiting at the Lake

This past year, the clutter and crowds of Southern California finally got to me, and I was longing for a spacious place. I needed to just get away. Someplace simple. Someplace sane. Someplace quiet where I could reconnect with my Maker. What a blessing, then, when some friends from our church asked us to vacation with them for a week at Lake Almanor in Northern California.

When the time came to leave, I was anxious to get into the fresh mountain air and be in the midst of God's creation so I could hear His voice again.

When we arrived at the quiet community, the pine tree-lined roads, the peaceful lake, and the groups of deer here and there on the front lawns of the homes all represented a vastly slower pace of life. A pace of life I was longing to experience.

The first morning at the lake, I got up early and walked down Peninsula Drive all the way to its end—a place called Peaceful Point—a small expanse of beach where you can watch the sun rise up as if it were coming right out of the lake. I got there about the time the sun's rays were hitting the water. *Here is my spacious place*, I thought as I sat on a bench with not a soul around and waited to hear God speak. But as I sat in the silence, there was nothing. No voice from heaven. No vision from God. No warm fuzzy feeling. Just silence. I asked God for something in the quietness—a quiet word from Him to my heart, a clear direction about where He wanted to lead me, sudden inspiration about what I was to write in this book. But still there was nothing.

I realized then that it had been a long time since I'd just come to Him and sat in His presence. So long, that just sitting with Him in the silence seemed awkward, like running into an old friend and not knowing what to say, or where to start, and feeling guilty for not keeping in touch. Perhaps God wanted to teach me how to just be alone and quiet with Him, not expecting anything, not looking to take anything away, but instead giving of my time and self to just *be* with Him—which I hadn't done for a while. Maybe He wanted me to just sit with Him like I'd sit with a best friend on a bench in the quiet cool of the morning. I realized then that as much as I missed my quiet times of being alone with God in a spacious place, He missed them even more. As I had gotten busy and let my life rush into overtime, He still waited for me to meet with Him. That thought saddened me. At the same time, it made me want to be with Him all the more.

For that, I would wait with Him in the quiet, whether He chose to speak to me or not.

So I continued to sit there in the quiet with Him until the sun had risen and the world around me had woken up. As I walked away from Peaceful Point I whispered, "I'll come back again, Lord. And we'll just sit. And even if You choose not to speak, I'll still come."

By the third morning, it didn't matter whether God said anything or not. We were together, the Lord and me, in a spacious place. And my heart was, once again, at home.

Jesus, too, often had to withdraw from the commotion and the crowds to rest His body, reconnect with His Father, refresh His heart.

Living in the Quiet Place

I can recall times when my husband and I have been so wiped out by the stress and pace of life around us that sometimes we just want to sit in the quiet. Granted, that comes easier for him than me. Most of the time, I want to fill in the space with my words, as if our conversation is what makes the time together special. I've since learned that just being together, in the quiet, can bond our hearts together. And it is sometimes what my husband prefers—to get me to slow down and be quiet and ready to hear what he has to say. I suppose my Lord is not much different. How He'd like for me to get quiet and wait for Him so that when He's ready to speak, I'll be ready to hear what He wants to say.

Funny how we often seek out those spacious places away from the commotion and the crowds in order to be with someone we love, so that we can tune out everything else and just concentrate on the one we're with, the one we love, the one whose voice we want to hear more than anything else in life.

Jesus, too, often had to withdraw from the commotion and the crowds to rest His body, reconnect with His Father, refresh

His heart. It's interesting that He chose places like the Sea of Galilee, the Mount of Olives, and the Garden of Gethsemane to be alone. He must have longed for a spacious place as well where He could talk to His Father, drink in the quiet, and gain strength for His next task.

Finding Your Spacious Place

Most of us can't just drive to the mountains, vacation at the lake, or go find a quiet park when our hearts are crying out for a spacious place with God. So we must learn how to "go away" with Him in our hearts and find that spacious place with Him even in the midst of a hectic life.

Although I was in the first-class section of the airplane before I noticed my spacious place, I could have just as easily found it in coach, or in a chair back at the crowded airport. Remember the tale of the two sisters in chapter 3? Martha felt cornered and stressed in her crowded kitchen, but Mary was able to find her wide-open space in the living room. Both women were in the same house, surrounded by the same circumstances, but in two different states of mind. Two different locations of the heart. It was a matter of perspective...and a matter of mental and spiritual location. Martha was busy with the details of life at that moment. Mary was in the next room, fully aware of the presence of Jesus.

Finding our spacious place involves going away with Him in our hearts, leaving the distractions of this world, and focusing on the Lord—right where we are in life. We can do that by practicing each of these steps, which, when put together, spell REST:

Realize that He is in control and you are not

Martha's feeling that she had to do it all may have contributed to her stress and her feeling of being cornered in the kitchen. My insistence on getting home according to my schedule led to the frustration and feeling of being trapped at O'Hare Airport. When we acknowledge that God is in control and we are not, that is the first step in climbing out of the race car driver's seat and letting God determine the pace that we travel. Suddenly the speed at which we're traveling doesn't matter as much because we realize who is at the helm. And being with Him is suddenly far more important than getting where we were trying to go.

Expect Him to come through

Not only is God in control, He also has a plan. He wants to take you there and perhaps even surprise you with it, so expect the best. Sometimes we can mentally acknowledge God is in control, but we still act as if He won't do anything. "Okay, I guess this is what He wants," we may concede. But then, wouldn't He be far more pleased if we waited expectantly for Him to come through? The expectation causes us to look for His deliverance and experience His peace in the waiting.

Surrender your strategy

When I devise the plan, I'm still acting like I'm in control. Sometimes I actually *pray my plan* to God, as if He hasn't thought up as good of a plan as I have! But there is rest in saying, "God, I don't have the solution, but I know *You* do." (Remember how my prayer of surrender shortly preceded my upgrade to first class?)

Trust in His next step

Remember the lesson from chapter 5? To rest is to trust. And by trusting our next step to God, we have already begun to relax our shoulders and wait upon Him in faith. As I boarded that airplane, I knew in my head (but had yet to experience it) that His plan to get me home was going to be far better than my original plan. And boy, was it!

Protecting Your Space

As we endeavor to find that spacious place, every day, in our hearts, we'll need to protect it—at all costs. I've found that getting busy isn't hard to do. Getting hemmed in and overwhelmed comes naturally. But setting up barriers around your time and space—so your time with God doesn't get overrun—now *that's* a skill. I've set a few ground rules in my life to keep my schedule sane so I don't wake up one day to find myself in the overwhelmed zone again. Granted, the unexpected comes up every now and then, and I must decide if it's worth being flexible. But for the most part, these principles have served me well in putting boundaries or hedges around my time and margin back into my life:

- Plan ahead so you won't be away from home more than a certain number of evenings per week. I choose to not be away from home more than two evenings a week, unless it's a prearranged situation with my family. I've found that the less time I'm away from home, the less tension there is between me and my husband, the less my daughter feels neglected, and the less I feel behind on the household chores. If a third evening creeps up and it's something I really want or need to do, I first see what else can be moved, then I check with my family for their response.

- Plan "margin" into your day. In other words, don't back up appointments next to each other or leave so little time between your obligations that you force yourself to run late and therefore stress yourself out. Pad your day with slots of open time that will help you feel as if you're living in a more spacious place. Sometimes the best parts of my day are the open spaces I planned into my schedule so I could sit in my car a few extra minutes and read while I wait for my daughter to get out of school, and so on.

- Don't worry about what will happen tomorrow. Worry closes us in and makes us feel trapped.

- Don't regret what happened yesterday. There's nothing more claustrophobic than trying to get back yesterday and finding you can't.

- Don't turn on the computer and check email *before* you've made the time to converse with God. (This can really cramp up your day, I've discovered!)

- Pace yourself by starting your day with worship. That way you'll start the day with the right perspective, and won't feel as if the day is continually slipping away.

Song of a Spacious Life

Here is a song from the Bible that may inspire you as you long for and begin to find that spacious place in your life. Drink up these words from David, who wrote them in the Judean wilderness. They are surely the words of someone who has met God in a spacious place:

> God—you're my God!
>> I can't get enough of you!
> I've worked up such hunger and thirst for God,
>> traveling across dry and weary deserts.
>
> So here I am in the place of worship, eyes open,
>> drinking in your strength and glory.
> In your generous love I am really living at last!
>> My lips brim praises like fountains.
> I bless you every time I take a breath;
>> My arms wave like banners of praise to you.
>
> I eat my fill of prime rib and gravy;
>> I smack my lips. It's time to shout praises!
> If I'm sleepless at midnight,
>> I spend the hours in grateful reflection.
> Because you've always stood up for me,
>> I'm free to run and play.
> I hold on to you for dear life,
>> And you hold me steady as a post.
>
>> (Psalm 63:1-8 THE MESSAGE)

Do you long for that kind of peace and liberty? Do you want to be able to say, like David did, "I'm in the place of worship, eyes open, drinking in your strength and glory"? Do you long to echo his words, "I'm free to run and play"? That kind of liberty comes from living in a spacious place with your God where there is ample time and room to dwell upon Him and grow in your relationship with Him.

The next time you're feeling hemmed in, cry out to God for your spacious place. And then wait upon Him as He takes you there, in your heart.

Clearing Out a Spacious Place

WHICH OF THE FOLLOWING space stealers do you need to be most aware of, and why?

Having to have something—now!

Work that presses in on you

Drivenness

Which of the steps in REST (pages 121–22) present to you the most challenge, and why?

How will you meet those challenges in order to create your spacious place?

Which of the ways to "protect your space" (on pages 123–24) will you incorporate into *your* life?

Memorize Psalm 18:19 as a personal encouragement and reminder to look for your spacious place every day. (Write the verse here—it's a short one, and just writing it will help you begin to memorize it.)

Intimacy with God and continuous noise are mutually exclusive. If there are to be times of conscious intimacy with Him, there must be times of silence and solitude. God will not shout over the clamor of our lives.

STEVE McVEY

NINE

Choosing to Live
a Simpler Life

I'VE BEEN A COLLECTING ADDICT for as long as I can remember. At age five, it was Raggedy Ann dolls. Then it was cat figurines. By the time I was 10 or 12, I was collecting just about anything I came across: polished rocks, stamps, marbles, postcards. Believe it or not, I even collected bubble-gum-wrapper comics!

But in my adult years, I've limited my collection to Cinderellas. Dolls, ornaments, figurines, and clocks take up every bit of space in two seven-foot-high curio cabinets in my bedroom. They remind me that I married a prince, and that my dreams and wishes have come true. And because most of them have been gifts, they also remind me of people who love me.

But collecting stuff has not only hemmed me in and kept me from a spacious place, it has interfered with my heart, too. You see, it took a 5.0 earthquake near my home to open my eyes and convict my heart about where my treasure was…and how my life needed to be simplified.[1]

Misplaced Treasure

It was the middle of the night, four years ago, when I awoke from an earthquake jolt. I jumped out of bed and ran to one of the curio cabinets. With feet apart and both hands out in front of me, I prepared to brace my body against the 150-pound cabinet to keep it from falling over should the shaking increase. As the house stilled, I remembered my then-six-year-old daughter, who was sleeping soundly near a shelf that could have toppled onto her! And I thought of my husband, who was still dreaming beneath a large picture frame that now hung crooked. And there I was protecting Cinderella! My concern for my collection had outweighed my concern for my own family. My "treasure" had gotten a little out of hand.

I realized then that to live in a spacious place—mentally, emotionally, spiritually, and physically—my "hold" on things had to go. And for me to live a life in which my heart is at rest, my heart had to be free—free of clutter, free of anything I love more than my God.

Jesus said in Matthew 6:19-21, "Do not store up for yourselves treasures on earth, where moth and rust destroy, and where thieves break in and steal. But store up for yourselves treasures in heaven, where moth and rust do not destroy and where thieves do not break in and steal. For where your treasure is, there your heart will be also."

How good it would feel, I thought, *not to worry that an earthquake—or fire or robbery—would destroy my treasures.*

Keeping It Simple

When my husband and I first married, we had few possessions of value. And you know what? We didn't worry about a thing when we were vacationing or away from home all day. If someone were to break into our one-bedroom apartment (and we lived in an area where it happened quite often), we wouldn't lose much. There was literally nothing worth taking. Some old furniture. A few basic appliances. Nothing costly. Nothing valuable. Somehow, it was comfortable to live so simply.

Yet today I worry that my Cinderella collection will break the next time another 5.0 or higher quake rolls in. I fear my computer, DVD player, or laptop might be taken the next time I forget to lock the back door.

Jesus' advice in Matthew 6 was practical, as well as spiritual. To store up treasures in heaven rather than in my home means I never have to worry that they'll break or be stolen or destroyed. And treasures in heaven will greet me someday when I arrive; my trinkets on earth will not.

Collecting the Right Treasures

In our desire to live freely and lightly we must think about collecting heavenly treasures rather than earthly treasures, which hem us in and compete for our hearts. Heavenly treasures are the things that will last forever. According to Scripture, only two things are eternal: God's Word (Isaiah 40:8) and people (Revelation 22:5).

How do I invest in God's Word? By studying it, applying it, memorizing it, teaching it, allowing it to transform my life.

And how do I invest in people? By loving them, showing Christ to them, discipling them in the faith, helping them turn from a life of sin, having a hand in transforming their lives.

Such investments are spiritual and often cannot be displayed here on earth. In fact, the more we let God do the accounting and displaying, the more we have that we probably didn't realize!

So how do we store up heavenly treasures rather than earthly things? Here are some ideas of what we can collect:

- All the fruit of the Spirit (Galatians 5:22-23)

- Scripture verses you have memorized (Psalm 119:11)

- People with whom you've shared the gospel (Mark 16:15)

- Children you've loved and cared for, or widows you've "adopted" as grandmas (James 1:27)

- Leaders you've trained in ministry (2 Timothy 2:2)

- New believers you've helped usher into the kingdom and disciples who've learned to walk with God from your instruction and example (Matthew 28:19-20)

- Lives that have been touched by your encouragement (Ephesians 4:29)

- Worn-out, read-through, marked-up Bibles full of your own study notes (2 Timothy 2:15)

These kinds of treasures won't take up a lot of room on a shelf or demand your time in maintenance. And they're not items that can be stolen or destroyed, either. Plus, they'll store up for you an investment in the kingdom of God.

Clearing Out the Clutter

God wants us to live freely and lightly, remember? So we must let Him clear out of our lives the baggage that holds our hearts down, the clutter that crowds in around us, the weight that keeps us from running so we *can* live freely and lightly. Psalm 119:32 says, "I run in the path of your commands, for you have set my heart free." But what needs to go so our hearts—and lives—can truly be free? What needs to be cleared out of the corners and stripped off of us so that we can live in a spacious place with room to worship, pray, rest, and play?

For me, deciding *not* to buy one more Cinderella set my heart free. I realized I *can* live without the clutter. For you, it may mean letting go of something else that takes your time, your space, or your peace of mind.

Losing the Weight

Hebrews 12:2 tells us to "strip off every weight that slows us down, especially the sin that so easily hinders our progress. And let us run with endurance the race that God has set before us. We do this by keeping our eyes on Jesus, on whom our faith depends from start to finish" (NLT).

For me, the weight that slows me down the most is having *too many things*. Too many appointments in my schedule. Too many obligations on my plate. Too many clothes in my closet. And too many Cinderellas on my shelves.[2] Therefore, I have to constantly remind myself to "strip off" the things that can easily distract me or deter me from being with God and living a simple, uncluttered, uncomplicated life.

Charles Swindoll calls it "reordering your private world" and says "everything around us works against reordering and simplifying our lives. Everything! Ours is a cluttered, complicated world. God did not create it that way. Depraved, restless humanity has made it that way!"[3]

"To reorder one's own world, the need to simplify is imperative," Swindoll says. "Otherwise we will find ourselves unable to be at rest within, unable to enter the deep, silent recesses of our hearts, where God's best messages are communicated. And if we live very long in that condition, our hearts grow cold toward Christ and we become objects of seduction in a wayward world. What perils await us in that condition."[4]

Collecting Memories over Material Goods

I mentioned earlier that shortly after Hugh and I married, we lived simply and didn't have much. During that time, we determined we would not spend a lot of money collecting things (most of the Cinderellas came from other people, by the way!), but we would invest in experiences instead, like traveling to exotic places, making family memories, participating in activities that were out of the ordinary. At first that was easy. We had so little money during our early married years that we *couldn't* collect anything—and we couldn't travel to exotic places, either! But even then, God blessed those years that we were living simply. Because I worked for a newspaper, we were given complimentary press passes to several of Southern California's amusement parks a couple times a year, and we had unique opportunities for

VIP seats at places like Laguna Beach's Festival of Arts' "Pageant of the Masters." I even got Hugh, a sci-fi fanatic, into one of the biggest Star Trek conventions ever held because of a story I wrote on "Trek Mania." We also had several used cars *given* to us during those years, as well as several living room couches, a practically new bedroom set, and even a big-screen TV!

But in recent years, as we've become able to afford more, we've had to constantly remind ourselves of what's important and what will last so we don't end up collecting material possessions instead of memories. For example, instead of buying each other gifts for our 15-year wedding anniversary, we sailed as a family to the Bahamas with my parents, my two brothers, and their families. The memories of that cruise alone—telling hilarious stories at the dinner table every night, spending a day together in Nassau, snorkeling on a white-sand beach, and (my husband's favorite) watching *Pirates of the Caribbean* on opening night on a ship that was actually sailing in the Caribbean!—were worth more than a lifetime of possessions. Those memories cannot hold a price. They also can't be broken, stolen, or destroyed.

Time to Simplify

So how can you begin to de-clutter and make a spacious place around you where little else but what's important takes your time? How can you simplify your life in a way that brings rest and peace? How can you live more simply so that you, too, can experience rest rather than worry and collect experiences rather than more stuff?

Simplify Your Schedule—Ask yourself, "What can go?" Some families have a policy that their children can each have one extracurricular activity at any given time. So if Johnny wants to play soccer, he may have to give up piano for a season. And if Andrea wants to be in gymnastics, she may have to pass on cheerleading and dance. My daughter, at ten years old, had never been more stressed out than when we had her in cheerleading, dance, piano, and Awana—all at the same time, along with a demanding course load in school. I should've seen it coming when she wanted to join the cheerleading squad in addition to her other three activities. But since Awana was church-related, her dance group was a ministry, and her piano lessons were building in her a skill, we didn't want to drop any activities. But that fourth activity pushed her over the brink. I didn't realize it until she told me one night, in tears, that she *hated* her life. "Why?" I asked her. "I have too many things I have to do," she complained. The next day, we pulled her off the cheerleading squad and out of piano. Simplifying her life caused her grades to go back up and her moods to even out. We've all learned since that carrying too much on our plates simply isn't worth the time or trouble. We also learned a valuable lesson about what our daughter could and could not handle. If her parents pushed her, she performed. But if we let her rest, she gladly took that as well. We saw it was far more healthy for her to put off all the activities for a year or two and just focus on resting and enjoying life as a fifth grader rather than to be involved in everything and be continually stressed out. If your kids are busy, you're busy. But you know what? If you're not liking the rush and pace of it all, chances are they're not liking it, either.

God will bless us when we reorder our lives and clean up the clutter in our hearts as well as in our homes.

Sort Through Your Stuff—It's amazing how much lighter and freer I feel when I have less stuff. Every year or so my husband insists I go through my closets and get rid of whatever I haven't worn in the past year. "If you haven't worn it in a year, you're not going to wear it again," he says. Hugh is a tosser. Primarily because his parents were keepers. He grew up surrounded by *so much stuff* that he feels a liberating pleasure in throwing things away.

My daughter must be the same way. When I helped Dana pack up most of the dolls and princess items she'd collected during the first ten years of her life, it was amazing how less stressed she became. Not that the dolls and all the princess things arranged neatly on her shelves had caused her stress. But de-cluttering the room and leaving some good old open space did wonders to her whole countenance. There were wide open spaces in the corners, not stacks of books and toys all over the floor. Her desk had rhyme and reason, not a billion knickknacks she had to keep organized. I realized, regrettably, that I'd given her far more than she could manage while she was younger, and was constantly on her case to keep it all neat. But she never wanted all that. She wanted to live simply, bless her heart. She wanted to live a simple and spacious life!

God will bless us when we reorder our lives and clean up the clutter in our hearts as well as in our homes. When we ask for His guidance in helping us to live simply, He convicts our hearts about the nonessentials and gives us wisdom to decide what needs to go and what can stay. Like with our knickknacks and extra clothing, the things He tells us to throw away are seldom missed. Rather, we end up enjoying life more because we have some space around us again...and less stuff holding on to our hearts.

Stay Within the Lines—When we go outside the lines and leave no margin in our life, that's when we begin to feel over-whelmed and out of control. Add margin to your life (as I men-tioned in the last chapter) by consciously not taking on more than you know you can handle. Prioritize your life by putting God first, family second, work or ministry third. I've found that when I put God first, my need for my own personal time is often met during my time with Him because of the way He refreshes me in our times together. Plus, God honors my time with Him in the mornings by giving time back to me at the end of the day for exercise, extra time with Dana, some meaningful time with Hugh, or some time for recreation or relaxation. Putting margin in your life also means committing *only* to what you can do, rather than *anything* you can do. For example, if someone else can just as easily volunteer to head up the PTA fundraiser, let them. But if a task calls for a skill or ability you alone happen to have and you are feeling called to do it, then go for it! If you love to do it, and God wants you to do it, joy and energy will result from doing it.

By limiting yourself to only what you do well, and what your family or others need you to do, within reason, you are placing margin around your personal time and saving it for where it's most needed, most effective, and for the most part, most appreciated. That glorifies God, too. Because more than anyone else, He wants you doing what He created you to do, not running around here and there doing *everything* and leaving little time left for Him.[5]

Considering It All Rubbish

One of the most perplexing—and disturbing—statements Jesus ever uttered was His response to a rich man who inquired of Him how to inherit eternal life. When Jesus recited to him five of the commandments, the man said he had kept them all since childhood. So Jesus added the clincher: "Sell everything you have and give to the poor, and you will have treasure in heaven. Then come, follow me" (Luke 18:22). Wow...why did Jesus make it so difficult for the man to follow? Who of us could do such a thing? And did Jesus really mean for him to sell *everything* he had? Jesus' followers responded as I would have when they heard this exchange and, in astonishment, asked, "Who then can be saved?" Jesus replied by saying, "What is impossible with men is possible with God" (verses 26-27).

Some Bible teachers explain that Jesus knew the man's heart and therefore asked him for what was most important to him in order to prove a point. The lesson, then, is that we should get rid of anything that has become more important than God, or anything that gives us our security and identity, so that we are fully dependent on God for all of that. But still, I must ask myself, in light of that story, would I be willing to give up *everything* I have today to follow Him?

Perhaps Jesus' words to me in my situation today might be, "Give up all your titles and all your ambitions and everything you think you must do to please Me or to feel good about yourself, and just follow Me."

Perhaps what He would say to you is, "Give up those things around you that make you feel safe and secure and just trust in Me." Or maybe He would say, "Get rid of the peripheral activities in your life that keep you so busy and spend some time in the quiet getting to know Me. When you find Me, you will discover who *you* are as well."

The apostle Paul, in Philippians 3, said he had a lot around him to make him feel safe and secure and of value. He said he had more reason than anyone to put confidence in himself. He had a great Jewish lineage, he was schooled in the Scriptures, he was blameless in keeping all the religious rules. But he renounced it all. He said none of it mattered anymore once he came to know Christ. Paul said, "Whatever was to my profit I now consider loss for the sake of Christ. What is more, I consider everything a loss compared to the surpassing greatness of knowing Christ Jesus my Lord, for whose sake I have lost all things. I consider them rubbish, that I may gain Christ and be found in him..." (verses 7-9). Now there is a man who knew what it meant to live simply and keep his focus!

Paul was saying that to know God meant so much more than the titles and reputation and accomplishments he had collected the first part of his life, so he wasn't going to invest any more time in what ultimately didn't matter. Now that I'm getting older, I am beginning to understand that mentality. How many more *things* will I collect that will someday burn? How much time will

I invest working for titles and reputations and people's admiration, which the book of Ecclesiastes says are all "meaningless" and "fleeting"? Or will I start throwing off what hinders me and spend the rest of my days living simply, and walking unhindered, and living uncluttered?

Paul was instructing us to do the same: Don't spend your days collecting things. Instead, get to know the Maker of all things. Don't worry about your résumé. Live for the Resurrected One. Don't stress over your schedule. Instead, live peacefully in the hands of the One who has ordained—and counted—your days.

Time to Let It Go

Ironically, as I was finishing up this chapter, the most devastating wildfires in California's history blazed through much of San Diego County, consuming nearly a half million acres of land and destroying more than 3,000 homes in their wake. Friends from my church and neighbors were nervously watching their property lines and keeping an eye on the blazing hills within short miles of their homes. In the midst of the firestorms, the same question crossed all of our minds: If we get the notice to evacuate during the night, what will we take with us? What is absolutely irreplaceable? Interestingly, none of us packed suitcases of *things*. None of us worried about all the *stuff* we'd lose. Most of us just set our picture albums by the door, kept our family nearby, and waited. After all, most of what we have will burn in the end anyway.

During those nights when we were instructed to stay indoors and listen for evacuation warnings, I slept with incredible peace, knowing that the most important things in my life—my relationship with God, my peace of mind from knowing Him, my family's eternal security in Him—can never be taken away...not by fire, flood, or frenzy.

It's in times like these that a simpler life—of having our true treasure in Him—brings incredible rest and peace.

$\mathcal{S}$*implifying for a Stress-Free Life*

F ROM THE LIST OF SUGGESTIONS on pages 131–32, which *eternal things* would you like to start collecting? Can you think of a few more that are not included in that list?

Why not set a goal now of how you will begin collecting what you listed above?

Reflect on the following verses. Next to each one, note how that verse represents living a simple, uncluttered, and spacious life (I did the first one for you):

> Psalm 37:4—If I am delighting myself in God, I will not be running after "things."

> Psalm 119:11—

> Psalm 119:32—

> Psalm 119:45—

Matthew 6:19-21—

Philippians 3:7-11—

Spend some time presenting your heart and home before God. What is He impressing upon your heart that needs to go so you can "run in the path" of His commands (Psalm 119:32)? List here the things that need to go...

From your schedule:

From your home:

From your heart:

What is the price of silence but the gift of self to God? It is to shut our eyes to what the world considers important and listen only to the Holy Spirit's call.... O how rare it is that the soul is sufficiently stilled to let God speak.

FRANÇOIS FENELON

TEN

Shining like Stars
in a Nighttime Sky

LACY BEAMED WITH A RARE BEAUTY. At first I figured it was her youth. This 22-year-old student at Mississippi College had lived a lot less years, spent a lot less time in the sun, and apparently saw a lot less stress in her life than me. Yet I couldn't help but feel there was something *more* to her radiance than youth. When we spoke about which songs she should sing at the conference to introduce and close my speaking sessions, I saw a humility in her that was rare for one her age. But when Lacy walked on stage to lead the women in worship, she came alive. Was it any wonder that one of the songs she sang so beautifully was one she wrote and titled "Just Rest"?

"I was having a real tough week a while back with some schoolwork that was piling up, some intense projects that were due, and some things happening in my personal life," Lacy told the group of women. "As I was sitting at my desk, I started to pray about how overwhelmed I felt about everything. And His words came so sweetly: Just rest."

Then Lacy sang a song of praise to her Maker for the rest He pours into our life when we acknowledge that He's the Potter, and we're still in His hands.[1]

Sweet Lacy McNeil had been with God. And it showed.

Transformation Time

When people are with God, they're changed, transformed.

When Moses came down from the mountain after having been with God for 40 days, his face shone so brightly with the glory of God the people insisted that he wear a veil. Moses had been with God, and it showed (Exodus 34:29-35).

In 2 Chronicles 15:1-9, we read that large numbers of people came to Israel to be near King Asa "when they saw that the Lord his God was with him." This king had the reputation of one who had been with God. The prophet Azariah even told Asa, "The Lord is with you when you are with him." Asa had been with God, and it showed.

Have you ever thought about that being *your* legacy? *She had been with God, and it showed.*

We can try to put on our best Christian face and say all the right words and do all the right things, but we are not truly transformed by Him until we have spent time in His presence. We can attempt to live maturely and grow through our circumstances, but until we've spent time at His feet, the transforming work cannot be done. And for us to shine as Moses did, and have the reputation that Asa had, we must come to know the Lord as they did.

The apostle Paul urged the Philippians (and us, as well) to live so obediently and therefore so differently from the rest of the world "so that you may become blameless and pure, children of God without fault in a crooked and depraved generation, in which you *shine like stars* in the universe as you hold out the word of life..." (Philippians 2:14-16).

I am convinced that when you and I have taken the time to sit at God's feet, to be refreshed and refueled by Him, we will shine like stars in the nighttime sky, against the dark backdrop of a world that rushes by. That's because anybody can be busy these days. But it takes someone surrendered—someone committed to God, someone who numbers their days, someone who trusts in the Lord and His work on their behalf—to slow down and live differently. In doing so, we can't help but stand out from the rest of the world and *"shine like stars* in the universe."

A woman who spends time with God is a woman who has more wisdom and insight from being schooled in the presence of God. She's a woman who has more depth of character because she's been refined through silent times with God. She's a woman who stands apart from others because of the One she has been with. And she's one who shines with a radiance because of the Pure Light with whom she fellowships.

I want to be seen that way and known that way. Therefore, I must live that way. But it all comes down to whom I'm with and how much time I'm willing to spend with Him.

It's Not About Us

It's all about Him. There are times, however, when I slip and think it's all about me.

This past year, I had to rebuild the women's ministry in my church from the ground up. A leadership transition in my church had caused several of my key leaders—and good friends—to leave the church, leaving me with several vacancies and the feeling that I couldn't move forward. Some people tried to encourage me in the midst of this difficult circumstance, but I was feeling downright debilitated at the loss of some of my best friends and leaders.

About the same time, I had been asked by a large church in the Midwest to come present a one-day women's conference. "And by the way, can you come in the day before and speak to our women's leadership team?" the women's ministry director asked. "They need some motivation, and I'm sure you'd have so much to offer them."

They *need some motivation?* I thought. *And they are hoping to get it from* me?

Since I tend to err on the side of complete transparency, I told the women's director the first thing that came to my mind, and the main concern that had been weighing on my heart.

"To be quite honest, I really don't think I have *anything* to offer your leadership team right now," I said, apologetically. "You see, I'm in the middle of a transition with my own women's ministry and I've been feeling so disqualified to lead lately and I've been struggling with motivation myself. Besides, you direct the women in a church of 3,000, and I'm the director of women in a church of only 200. How could I possibly have something to offer *your* women?"

But my new friend's words cut sharply into my soul.

"Cindi, I haven't met you, but one of our women drove to Indianapolis to hear you speak over the summer, and she was so touched by your heart for God and what you shared about the struggles you were going through that we wanted you here to touch our hearts as well. We're not asking you to speak because of your résumé or the size of your church, but because you've been with God."

There it was! It wasn't about me or what I could do. It was all about *who I knew.*

I wept after that phone conversation. I wept at the gentle rebuke my heavenly Father had given me because I had dared to think my ministry was all about what I had or didn't have to offer. I wept at the thought of His grace in gently reminding me that I could continue to do what I'd done in the past because He would continue to work through me. And I wept at the thought that *anyone* would be able to see from my life (especially lately) that I'd been with God. In the midst of the tears that day, I found a new strength to continue ministering, in spite of what I felt I was losing around me. I had the Lord going before Me, and I was soon ready to shine for my Maker once again.

Remaining in Him

Could it be that our quiet time with God is the only redeeming factor that makes any of us pleasing or presentable to others? Could it be that our alone time with Him is the sole source of our receiving anything useful to offer to others? Jesus said in John 15:4, "Remain in me and I will remain in you. No branch can bear fruit by itself; it must remain in the vine. Neither can you bear fruit unless you remain in me."

When I have *not* been sitting at the feet of Jesus, when I have *not* been in His Word, when I have *not* gone to Him to refuel and refresh me, I have literally nothing to offer.

The best thing—or make that the only thing—I have going for me is God. Time with Him. The relationship with Him. A love for Him. When He slips out of the picture (because I'm running too fast or have failed to prioritize my time with Him) or when He diminishes in my life (because I've cut my quiet time with Him down to a mere few minutes a day or nothing at all), I am nothing. And I have nothing to offer any one else as well. (Just ask my family!)

Beauty is the fruit of our relationship with God. Not stress. Or weariness. Or feeling overwhelmed.

The best thing you have going in *your* life is God. Time with Him. The relationship with Him. Remaining in Him. Apart from Him, you can do nothing...least of all, shine and shimmer.

Getting Our Beauty Rest

When I was thinking recently about where I'd end up in a few years if I didn't begin to slow down, I came across a line in a book that got me thinking long and hard about my direction in life: "The fruit of our love affair [with God] is our beauty; it is not something we can manufacture, manipulate or control."[2]

Whoa! That stopped me right in my tracks. *Beauty* is the fruit of our relationship with God. Not stress. Or weariness. Or feeling overwhelmed. If *beauty* is the result of our relationship with God, then the more we know Him and the more we grow with Him, the more beautiful—not busy—our heart and life will become.

I thought of my personal role models whom I've had the opportunity to meet over the past couple of years—women of faith who, despite demanding speaking and writing ministries, appear to model a lifestyle of peace and rest: Elisabeth Elliot, whose books discipled me from the time I was in high school, and who displays such maturity and wisdom; Cynthia Heald, whose Bible studies mentored me in my early years as a pastor's wife, and whose humble demeanor spoke volumes to me as a young author; Elizabeth George, who is able to write and speak more and more every year, but somehow manages to look more radiant and display more grace every time I talk with her. Each of those women have become more *beautiful* rather than more *busy* through the years. Each of them must know what it means to rest in the Lord. I want that "beauty rest" as well.

How can I, too, be a woman who grows closer to God through the years and not more haggard and tired from all the things I *do?* As I mentioned in the introduction of this book, it's not a question of external beauty and how to avoid the aging process. It's not a matter of image management. It's a matter of inner beauty and deep soul work—the kind that comes from sitting at God's feet and depending on Him, not my own efforts, to be a woman who is rested, rejuvenated, and refreshing to all around her.

Perhaps lovely Lacy had the right idea: Just rest.

Time to Shimmer

I love wearing glittery clothing. My husband says it's the high-school baton twirler in me. My youngest brother says it's because I'm an '80s girl. But I truly believe women should shimmer...all year long. We bring out glittery sweaters at Christmastime and New Year's Eve. When we wish to make a statement or feel special, we shimmer. But why not shimmer every day of the year as a reminder that we are to be set apart and shine like stars? My friend Ginny will put on the sparkles when she's feeling unusually down as a reminder to shimmer...even if she doesn't think she's sparkling.

"You are the light of the world—like a city on a mountain, glowing in the night for all to see," Jesus said to those who follow Him wholeheartedly. "Don't hide your light under a basket! Instead, put it on a stand and let it shine for all. In the same way, let your good deeds shine out for all to see, so that everyone will praise your heavenly Father" (Matthew 5:14-16 NLT).

Turning on the Light

In my book *When Women Walk Alone*, I suggest three steps for getting alone with God and infusing our lives with His light:

Sit at His Feet

This means basking in His presence, worshiping Him, getting quiet enough to hear Him speak to our hearts. It means letting the world rush by while we rest in Him.

In Mark 1:35, we read about how Jesus rose early in the morning while it was still dark and "went off to a solitary place, where he prayed." When His followers found out He was gone, they had a fit! They all went looking for Him, and when they found Him they said, basically, "What do You think You're doing? Everyone's looking for You. You have a job to do!"

When you, too, seek out a lonely place like Jesus did, chances are other people won't like to see you go. They'll want to give you something more to do, or spend time with you, or find you a date, or take you to the mall...anything but let you be alone. They mean well, of course, just as Jesus' friends meant well. But it's vital that we not let anything encroach upon our time alone with God.

Soak in His Word

When you spend time in God's Word, don't just read it. Swim in it, soak in it awhile, and get so deep into it that you find yourself drowning. I like to start in the Psalms, songs of such human emotion, and paraphrase them, making them personal songs of praise to Jesus. Then I'll spend time in study of some other portion of Scripture.

Another meaningful exercise is to go through the Gospels (Matthew, Mark, Luke, and John), reading about Jesus and closing your eyes and putting yourself in the scene. Ask yourself: What would I have said or how would I have felt if Jesus had said those words to me or touched me with His outstretched hand? Experience the stories by being there in your mind and heart. The Bible will come alive for you like it never has before!

Seek His Will

What does God want for your life? The only way you can know is by spending time with Him and His Word. In the Bible, God tells us a lot about how He desires for us to live. And when we pray, we can ask Him to help us view our lives, circumstances, and opportunities the same way He views them. It's when we gain His perspective on the world around us that we're most sensitive to His leading in our lives.

As you seek to do God's will, you'll find great fulfillment, for then you'll be living out His purpose in your life. And there's *nothing* you can do that's greater than that![3]

As you sit at God's feet, soak in His Word, and seek His will, His light will shine through you—a woman of rest and refreshment. And when you have His light *showing* through you and His power and love *flowing* through you, you'll stand apart in this world. So, you *glow* girl...shimmer on!

Standing Apart Through Stillness

WHICH OF THE FOLLOWING PRESENTS the most challenge to you, and why?

Sitting at His Feet—

Soaking in His Word—

Seeking His Will—

To succeed at something, we must have a plan. Prayerfully, think through how you will begin to sit before the Lord and let His light infuse your life. (For example, where will you go, what will you study, in what areas will you seek His will?) You may already be doing this. If so, great. If not, here's a great place to start. After praying it through, fill out the prayer of commitment on the next page.

My Prayer of Commitment

Lord, from this day forward I want to shine Your Light for all the world to see. I want to live at a pace that is refreshing to others, not draining on their spirits or on mine.

Lord, I will sit at Your feet by _____

_____

Lord, I will soak in Your Word by _____

_____

Lord, I will seek Your will in _____

_____

Signed: _____

Date: _____

You may see it over the margin and wistfully long to slip into that amazing Center where the soul is at home with God. Be very faithful to that wistful longing. It is the Eternal Goodness calling you to return Home, to feed upon green pastures and walk beside still waters and live in the peace of the Shepherd's presence. It is the life *beyond* fevered strain.

THOMAS R. KELLY

ELEVEN

Returning to the Joy of Simple Pleasures

WALKING THROUGH THE BEAUTIFUL GARDENS of the Huntington Library reminds me of how little of my time is spent in paradise-like places that make me long for heaven.[1] Breathing in the beauty, smelling the sweet aroma of roses, walking under the weeping willows, and listening to the "sounds" of silence not only make me homesick for heaven, but make me want to slow down and experience more lush, green gardens, perhaps as a way of preparing my heart for my future home.

We were made for the breathtaking beauty of Eden, to gaze at the wonders of a flower, watch the colors of a sunset, trace patterns in the clouds. Yet some of us only did that as children when the world, to us, was exciting and new.

When we slow down long enough to catch our breath and get out into a spacious place where we can sense the presence of God, we can be like children—experiencing this world as if it were, once again, exciting and new.

Glimpses of Paradise

I've seen very little of this world, regrettably. But some of the wonders I've seen and experienced have made my heart come alive and reinforced to me that I was made to experience a life of wonder, beauty, intimacy, and rest in a relationship with God. Walking along the shores of Cannon Beach, Oregon, at early tide made me think of the majesty of God and the magnitude of His power. Riding a bicycle through Wonder Valley in Central California reminded me of the joy of living lightly and freely. Strolling through the Rose Gardens in Portland, Oregon, and looking out over the city from atop Pittock Mansion under a full moon reminded me of the romance of God's love. Crossing the Bridge of the Gods over the Columbia River Gorge while surrounded by the Cascade Mountains and gazing at Bridal Veil Falls in Yosemite overwhelmed me with perspective that He is God and He is worthy of praise. All these experiences cause me to joyfully recite His Word, in praise: "O LORD, our Lord, how majestic is your name in all the earth!" (Psalm 8:1).

We've been given glimpses of heaven through the beauty of God's creation here on earth. Yet the Bible tells us "no eye has seen, no ear has heard, no mind has conceived what God has prepared for those who love Him" (1 Corinthians 2:9). As good as it gets here, there is going to be *so much more*. Living day by day with the knowledge that the best moments here on earth, the most beautiful places we can imagine, the most fulfilling days we've had are mere glimpses of the breathtakingly awesome experiences we'll have as we dwell with God in eternity is enough to take me away from the stress of everyday life and give me a higher perspective. My life is not about the rat race. It's not about work. It's not about *doing*. It's all about living for the One who created this world for me to enjoy *with* Him.

Life is about enjoying God and rejoicing in the simple pleasures of His creation. And I don't enjoy God's presence or His handiwork when I'm in a frenzy and overwhelmed with what I have to *do*. I enjoy Him when I repent of the pressured pace of life and turn to indulge, again, in my relationship with Him. I enjoy Him when I stop long enough to look out the window and see what He's left for me in the sky. I enjoy Him when I go away with Him in my heart in a poetic moment or dramatic pause in life...one that I like to think will make up a snapshot which God will someday roll out when He reviews how I lived and served Him on this earth.

Poetic Moments

I can recount some recent poetic moments in my life that caused me to return to the joy of simple pleasures, simple reminders of my Creator's love and eye for beauty.

I had forgotten how exquisite the sunsets are across the skies of the San Joaquin Valley in Central California, where I grew up. I had forgotten...until my daughter reminded me one afternoon when I was driving the country roads back home. I was heading from a book-signing event in Reedley back to my sister's house in Fresno, rushing to be back in time for dinner. My mind was on the events of the next day and all that I had to do that evening to prepare for them. I was so preoccupied that I saw only the road ahead of me.

Suddenly Dana, who was eight at the time, interrupted my thoughts: "Mom, *look* at that sunset!" she shrieked. Turning to my left, I saw the most breathtaking hues of pink, red, and blazing gold that I'd seen in a *long* time. The colors, forming a backdrop against the manicured rows of vineyards and agricultural pasturelands, created a majestic scene that momentarily left me speechless. Anything I could have said in that moment wouldn't have been enough.

But Dana said it all. "Isn't God a *great artist?*" she asked, still mesmerized with the display of color in front of her.

"Yes, Dana, He *is* a great artist," I replied softly. "And I bet He painted that there just for us tonight, to give us something beautiful to look at on our way home and to remind us to slow down and enjoy what He's created." Then it dawned on me: *Perhaps He put it there for* me...*to remind* me *to slow down.* After all, it took my young daughter's eyes to notice the sunset and point it out to me. In my total absorption on tomorrow, I could have so easily missed what He created for me that day.

I had also forgotten the simple pleasure of gazing at a rainbow.

As I was driving to my Jazzercise class late one afternoon, I was awestruck by a double-ended rainbow...one that stretched from one end of the sky to the other. It was the first time I'd ever seen such a sight. I reached for my cell phone to call my husband, to tell my daughter, to call *anyone* who would share the beauty of that moment with me. But then I realized that the Creator of that beauty was right there in the car with me. I put my phone down. "It's so beautiful," I whispered to Him as I continued staring at it, driving straight ahead. "Thank you, Lord." The quietness of the moment, spent just between the two of us, meant more than if I had gotten ahold of someone on the phone and just yakked about it.

And where I live, it's not difficult to forget the simple pleasure of fresh green grass. When my plane landed in Twin Falls, Idaho, one recent spring, I was amazed at the beauty of the lush, green grass everywhere I looked. Living in the concrete jungle of Southern California, I have to go to a park or someone's expansive and expensively landscaped home to see that much grass in one place. I've learned now, even when spotting a small patch of it, to slip off my shoes and enjoy the cool, soft carpet under my feet. Was this what it was like in the Garden, walking with God in the cool of the evening…feeling the lush green grass beneath one's feet and not having a care in the world?

What Have You Missed?

What is right in front of you that you've been too busy to notice? What grand gestures of God's love have you missed because your nose was in the paper, or your eyes were glazed over from weariness, or your mind was running full speed ahead?

Walking in the grass in the cool of the day, watching rainbows, admiring sunsets—they all represent the simple pleasures of life, before concrete was poured, before houses sprung up everywhere, before the pace of life picked up so much. These simple pleasures take me back to childhood days on my grandparents' farm or running through the sprinklers in my family's front yard on a hot summer day. And I'm reminded again that we were created for His pleasure. How it must please God when we stop and reconsider what He created and we enjoy our lives again with Him.

How it must please God when we stop and reconsider what He created and we enjoy our lives again with Him.

In his book *Celebration of Discipline*, author Richard Foster says we can live more simply—and more at peace—if we "develop a deeper appreciation for the creation. Get close to the earth. Walk whenever you can. Listen to the birds. Enjoy the texture of grass and leaves. Smell the flowers. Marvel in the rich colors everywhere. Simplicity means to discover once again that 'the earth is the Lord's and the fullness thereof' (Psalm 24:1)."[2]

Look Around at Creation

Jesus, being God in the flesh, came to earth to deliver (and live out) a message to us: God loves us more than we can fathom—and He found a way to redeem us for His own. Jesus must have known it would be difficult for us to remember that at times, or at least to keep a perspective about Him in the midst of our cluttered chaos. So He advised us to look around at what God made—on a daily basis—and watch for lessons on His love, pictures of His provision, and glimpses of His grace.

For instance, Jesus taught us to look at a flower and think of God's love, listen to a bird's song, and remember He will care for us. He taught us to stand in awe of a mountain and know that He is stronger and that through His power, we can do anything. He also taught us to look toward heaven and long for His return.

"Look at the lilies and how they grow," Jesus told His followers. "And if God cares so wonderfully for flowers that are here today and gone tomorrow, won't he more surely care for you?"(Luke 12:27-28 NLT). And if we missed it in the flowers, Jesus made sure we caught it by looking at the birds of the air: "Look at the ravens, free and unfettered, not tied down to a job description, carefree in the care of God. And you count far more" (Luke 12:24 THE MESSAGE). Just in case we still needed convincing, He told us, "Don't be afraid; you are more valuable to him than a whole flock of sparrows"(Matthew 10:31 NLT). Should we become intimidated or doubtful, He instructed us to look to the mountains for motivation: "If you have faith as small as a mustard seed you can say to this mountain, 'Move from here to there,' and it would move. Nothing will be impossible for you" (Matthew 17:20). Jesus' heavenly Father, centuries earlier, told us that when we need help, to look to the mountains as a means of gaining perspective on how high and mighty He is (Psalm 121:1-2).

Stay Alert for the Lessons

God not only wants us to slow down and smell the flowers, but also to go through life in somewhat of a contemplative and observant way so that we would notice what He has placed in this world so that we might gain wisdom and learn His ways. He tells us in Proverbs 6:5 to free ourselves from debt "like the gazelle from the hand of the hunter, like a bird from the snare of the fowler." He tells us to "go to the ant...consider its ways and be wise!" (verse 6) and in Proverbs 30 to be amazed at the "way of an eagle in the sky, the way of a snake on a rock, the way of a ship on the high seas" (verse 19). He tells us to be in awe of ants, who have little strength but work wisely; of locusts, who have no leaders but advance together in ranks; of a lizard, which can be caught yet dwells in kings' palaces (verses 25-27).

When we regain our sense of appreciation for what God has put in our path or placed around us, it keeps our minds ever learning, our hearts in a state of worship, and our souls in a state of rest. I can't help but think about how Jesus was constantly in touch with all that was around Him—a real nature person, if you think about it. Maybe it helped Him cope with being so far away from Home.

Jesus was born in a barn, baptized in a river, walked on water, prayed in the Garden, died on a hilltop, and ascended into the clouds. When He was feeling closed in, He arose early while it was still dark and found a solitary place (out in nature) to pray. He often took a boat out on the lake to collect His thoughts or have some quiet time away from the crowds. Other times He "withdrew...to a mountain by himself" (John 6:15). The earth was fully His and He experienced its simple pleasures with His heavenly Father. When you consider the incredible beauty of the Garden and world that surrounded Adam and Eve, you cannot help but realize God takes pleasure in our enjoyment of His creation. No wonder we like to walk through gardens, take a boat out on a lake, stand on the top of a mountain, or be out somewhere in nature to feel we are in His presence. Like Jesus, perhaps we, too, feel deep calling unto deep—our God calling out to us from the midst of what He's created—and cannot help but respond.

Psalm 19 bears testimony to God's presence in creation. Hear Him proclaiming who He is to us in our otherwise rushed lives:

> The heavens tell of the glory of God.
>   The skies display his marvelous craftsmanship.
> Day after day they continue to speak;
>   night after night they make him known.
> They speak without a sound or a word;
>   their voice is silent in the skies;
> Yet their message has gone out to all the earth,
>   and their words to all the world.
> The sun lives in the heavens
>   where God placed it.
> It bursts forth like a radiant bridegroom
>   after his wedding.
> It rejoices like a great athlete
>   eager to run the race.
> The sun rises at one end of the heavens
>   and follows its course to the other end.
>   Nothing can hide from its heat (NLT).

Psalm 19:6 in *The Message* tells us:

> That's how God's Word vaults across the skies
>   from sunrise to sunset,
> Melting ice, scorching deserts,
>   warming hearts to faith.

Rediscovering the Joy of His Presence

What if you, every day, sought pleasure and rest in the beautiful demonstrations of who God is by reading His Word across the skies and letting all He has created around you warm your heart to faith? Psalm 16:11 says, "In Your presence is fullness of joy; in Your right hand are pleasures forever" (NASB).

When we take time to be in His presence we experience true joy...no matter where we are and what is going on. And Psalm 139 tells us there's no place we can go where His presence is not, so it's a matter of opening our eyes and our hearts to rediscover the joy of being with Him wherever we are.

Satan's best tactic for getting us to forget God lies in getting us busy: Get us too busy to worship, too busy to laugh, too busy to enjoy life, too busy to be in His presence, too busy to notice the simple things that scream of the sovereignty of God. That kind of busyness is a sure-fire formula for a life of no joy. Don't let the enemy, or just life in general, rob you of the meaning of life—to love God and enjoy Him forever. That is what you will do throughout eternity. Get in shape for it by practicing it now. Remember the words of the psalmist? "Oh, how I wish I had wings like a dove; then I would fly away and rest! I would fly far away to the quiet of the wilderness" (Psalm 55:6-7 NLT).

Have *you* learned to fly away to that place in your heart where you are free to love Him, live with Him, breathe in His goodness, and relish in His love?

When you rediscover the simple pleasures of life—like looking for the lessons in the lilies, celebrating the beauty of sunsets, and listening for songs of praise from birds—you, too, will rediscover joy...and what it means to *fly far away* to that place of praise and rest.

$\mathcal{R}$ediscovering It All Again

LIST SOME SIMPLE PLEASURES you may have forgotten about (these might be activities you enjoyed as a child, places you visited long ago, or things you liked to watch):

Psalm 16:11 says in God's presence is "fullness of joy." Rewrite this verse a few times, substituting the words *In God's presence* for a simple pleasure in which you know He will join you (the first two are done for you):

1. As I gaze at a sunset (with Him) there is fullness of joy.

2. As I look for shapes in the clouds (and think of Him) there is fullness of joy.

3.

4.

5.

6.

According to the following verses, what are some of the simple pleasures in which you can find joy?

Psalm 84:4—

Psalm 107:29-30—

Psalm 127:4-5—

Psalm 147:1—

Ecclesiastes 3:22—

Ecclesiastes 5:19—

Ecclesiastes 9:7—

Write a prayer here to God, thanking Him for the simple pleasures He has given you and asking Him to open your eyes and reawaken your heart to the glimpses of Paradise He puts in your path every day. (As you learn to look for them, you will come to see more of His greatness and creativity through the variety of beauty in His creation…and you will develop a longing for your *real home.*)

There is a way of life so hid with Christ in God that in the midst of the day's business one is inwardly lifting brief prayers, short ejaculations of praise, subdued whispers of adoration and of tender love to the Beyond that is within.

THOMAS R. KELLY

TWELVE

Remaining in
the Secret Place

WHEN LUCY STUMBLED UPON an antique wardrobe and discovered within it the enchanting land of Narnia, she experienced such joy there she couldn't help but urge her closest friends and family to experience it with her. There was excitement, adventure, a whole world worth discovering by going to this dark closet and entering in. But what a shame it would've been if she couldn't have shared her experiences and the wonders of that secret place.

I can relate to Lucy in *The Lion, the Witch and the Wardrobe*, the first volume to C.S. Lewis' The Chronicles of Narnia. How can I experience the wonders and riches of rest that God has shown me through the door of surrender and not desire that others share in the experience as well? Of course, sometimes we like to keep "secret places" a secret. We fear that if too many other people know about them, those places won't be special anymore.

"Don't write about the lake in your book," my friend Paul told me with a smile after our families vacationed there together this past summer. "The fewer people who know about this place, the better." He wanted to guard that sanctuary so it would still be a quiet refuge for his family every summer. I can understand why (but not enough to keep from mentioning it in this book, I suppose!).

When it comes to discovering the doorway to a life of rest and peace—finding that hideaway in our heart where we can be with God and be revived, refreshed, and rejuvenated—how can we not share the blessing with others?

No one will be able to enter that personal inner sanctuary you share with God. But as you encourage others to enter into His rest, you will gain a network of friends and family who understand with you the treasure of a holy life rather than a harried one. And that will make your battle against busyness in your life that much easier.

Charles Swindoll, in his book *Intimacy with the Almighty*, says, "Those who determine to simplify their lives quickly discover it is a rigorous solo voyage against the wind."[1] But take heart. "If God is for us, who can be against us?" (Romans 8:31). We also know that "this is the confidence we have in approaching God (about finding our rest in Him and our change of lifestyle through His power): that if we ask anything according to his will, he hears us. And if we know that he hears us—whatever we ask—we know that we have what we asked of him" (1 John 5:14-15).

That's pretty clearly stated. If we ask God for the rest He longs for us to experience, we can be certain that He will provide it. *This is the resting place,* He continues to whisper to our hearts. *Come away with Me to a quiet place and get some rest.*

Shortly before He died, Jesus told His friends in John 16:12, "Oh, there is much more I want to tell you..." (NLT). Is that why He so desires for us to go away with Him? So He can reveal even more about Himself? Even more about His plans and purposes for our lives?

What more does He have to say to *you?* You will discover it as you continue to go away with Him in your heart. He will remain there, waiting for you. Watching and waiting in the living room of your heart. Waiting so He can tell you *so much more.*

On the days I don't meet with the Lord in the living room of my heart, He is still there, waiting for me. I know, now, that

I don't want to keep Him waiting. I want to know what He longs to tell me. I don't want Him to have to wait until I have time. I will *make the time* while there is still time. He will not run after me to spend that time with Him. Neither will He run alongside me, trying to keep up so He can get a word in, here and there. No, I must go to Him. I must go where He waits for me—in that secret, quiet place in my heart.

God recently, in His grace, gave me a reminder of how much He'd been waiting—and wanting—to be with me.

The Day the Doors Closed

It was one of those months that I talked about earlier, when I was speaking every weekend. When I was home, I was constantly in my study on my computer, writing talks, working on a book deadline, mothering my daughter during the distractions—existing, but not really living. I was putting my life in cruise control, pretty much not noticing anything or anyone around me, talking to God on the fly.

As I ran down the stairs one Saturday morning, off to a speaking engagement, I yelled to my daughter, on the way out the door, "Mommy will be home around three o'clock today and we'll do something together then, okay?"

I thought I heard her call "okay" just as I flew out the door.

A few hours later I forgot about that promise I made to Dana. That is, until I pulled into the driveway at about four o'clock that afternoon.

There on the garage door was a sign, scrawled in bright green marker, that said, "Welcome Home Mommy!!!"

And I realized that somebody had been missing me.

As I walked in, the house was unusually quiet and my daughter didn't pop her head around the door as she usually did when I got home. So I climbed the stairs and headed to my study to unpack my bags, fill out forms, and do all the paperwork that I do after speaking so that I could really "be at home." But as I rounded the corner at the top of the stairs, I noticed the door to my study was closed and there was a sign taped to it. It said, in the same bright green marker, "No study today! Too much hard work!"

So I turned around and headed to my bedroom, across the hall. But I stopped in my tracks when I saw that my bedroom door was closed as well. And taped to that door was a colorful note, created with my daughter's computer art program, which read,

> I love you, Mommy!!! I love your Chicken Inchiladias [someone had been scolded earlier for complaining about eating my chicken enchiladas]!!!! I love your hair, smile, clothes, face, and eyes!!!!!!
>
>   Love, Dana Katherine McMenamin

At that moment, I sensed a presence.

I turned and saw my Dana, with her arms and legs blocking the door of my study, eyes open wide with anticipation and a mischievous smile on her face as if to say, "Do you notice me now? Will you play with me now?"

I dropped my bags onto the floor, walked over to Dana, and knelt down. Hugging her tightly, I whispered into her ear, "Thank you, Dana. It means so much to Mommy to know that you want to spend time with me. I'm just so sorry you had to shut all the doors in front of me to get me to stop and notice you. The rest of the day is just ours, okay?"

Her grin told me that was the right response.

And in spite of all I had to do that evening, I didn't dare go into my study. I just left my bags right there in the hallway. And Dana and I went downstairs and played a favorite game of hers—over and over again. Then we cuddled up on the couch and watched a favorite movie of hers—one we had already seen over and over again. For the first time in a long while, I took the time to just *be* with her.

Who Is Missing *You*?

Dana opened my eyes to an important truth that day when she closed all the doors in front of me. She showed me not just that she won't be a child forever, and that I must seize these days to play with her while she still wants me around, but she also showed me that the one who loves me the most, the one I should love the most, was right in front of me, waiting to be noticed. And even though I was acknowledging now and then that she was around, she wanted more—she wanted to be the *focus* of my life.

I believe God feels the same way about us. We can get so busy that we put our relationship with Him in cruise control. We do things *for* Him, but not *with* Him. We talk to Him on our way out the door and promise to be with Him soon, but it doesn't happen. We get so caught up in activity that we fail to see that the One who loves us the most, the One who *we* should love the most, is right in front of us, waiting to be noticed.

God sometimes goes to the extreme of closing doors in front of us (like Dana did with me) to get us to stop and spend time with Him. Sometimes He puts a note right in our face—a portion of His Word, a convicting little story that's forwarded to your email in-box, an encouraging word from a friend—that says, in so many words, "I love you. I love your smile, your face, your eyes…I want to be with you. Will you notice Me now?"

Unlike our children, God doesn't *need* our attention. But He so much desires to be in a relationship with us—the kind of relationship in which we commune with Him daily, share with Him the secrets of our hearts, and live for Him fully. He doesn't want us to just acknowledge Him now and then. He wants to be the *focus* of our lives. In fact, He wanted that close relationship with us so much that He was willing to die so He wouldn't have to live without us (John 3:16).

How long has it been since He's had time with *you?*

Remaining in Him

Don't keep God waiting any longer. Meet with Him every day in the hideaway of your heart. Escape to your rendezvous with Him in the midst of the day, in the still of the night, throughout the course of your life. Rather than living in this world and looking for a spare moment to get away with God, think of your life, instead, as dwelling with Him and going away to visit the rest of the world with Him now and then. If you dwell there with Him, and visit the world now and then, you will know what it means to experience rest and to live in peace—God's peace for your otherwise overwhelmed life.

In chapter 2 of this book, I talked briefly of Enoch, who walked with God 300 years; of Abraham, who was called God's friend; of David, who was called a man after God's own heart and had the habit of waiting for God "more than watchmen wait for the morning." Each of those individuals knew of rest, waiting, and peace because they lived a life in which they abided in God. Jesus told us to remain in Him and He will remain in us (John 15:4). In the New American Standard translation of the Bible, Jesus tells us to "abide" in Him because we can do nothing without Him (John 15:5). To *abide* with Him means to dwell with Him and remain there, to make ourselves at home with Him, to live in a constant awareness of His presence. To have a conversation with Him that is ever flowing, thoughts of Him that are ever churning, whispers of praise for Him that are ever on our lips. That is what it means to abide, to dwell.

We can't dwell with God if we're constantly on the run.

We can't dwell with God if we're constantly on the run. To dwell with someone means to settle down and be at home with him. Oh to dwell with my God, rather than talk to Him while in a rush.

Finding the Balance

As we live in His presence, dwelling with Him daily, we will be in tune with Him and what He wants of our lives. He doesn't want us to just rest. We must live in the balance of a life of rest *and* service. When we are rested and refreshed by Him on a regular basis, we are able to serve with more power and effectiveness and have a greater impact on other's lives.

I have found that the days I am most effective as a servant of God are the days that I have first spent time with Him, resting in Him and receiving His strength to accomplish what He has for me to do. It is after time in His Word that my ears are more tuned to hear the cries of others He wants me to help. It is after time spent with Him in prayer that I see what He wants me to see, that I walk into those God-appointments that I probably would've missed had I started my day with busyness rather than being with Him. And then there are times when I am called to respond to a situation before I've had that planned time with God. On those days, when I know it's Him calling me to serve, I am confident the rest will follow in time.

As we rest in Him, He lets us know how He wants us to serve Him. And then He picks up the other end of that yoke and carries it with us so our work will not be burdensome, but a joy as He walks alongside us. A.W. Tozer said,

> To men and women everywhere Jesus says "Come unto me and I will give you rest." The rest He offers is the rest of meekness, the blessed relief which comes when we accept ourselves for what we are and cease to pretend. It will take some courage at first, but the needed grace will come as we learn that we are sharing this new and easy yoke with the strong Son of God Himself. He calls it "my yoke" and He walks at one end while we walk at the other.[2]

Sometimes the yoke is the burden of knowing we need to be alone with Him, but feeling frustrated because, at times, it just seems like it can't happen. Whatever you do, my friend, don't get discouraged or feel guilty when you cannot seem to carve out that alone time with God to the extent that you'd like to.

I have found that when my heart is burdened to be with Him, and I tell Him so, He often does what it takes to give me that alone time with Him. Remember, in His pursuing love of your heart and life, He wants that alone time with you even more than you want it with Him. If it's not happening due to circumstances beyond your control, cry out to Him, and He'll take you to that place Himself.

Guard Your Inner Sanctuary

Finally, my friend, once you've found your quiet place—that inner part of your heart that knows how to rest—guard it with all your heart. Return to it not just when you need to, but simply because you long to. Simply because *He* longs to meet you there. It is there that you will discover the treasures of knowing Him, and the purposes He has for your life. It is there that you will develop true authenticity and depth in your Christian life. It is there that you will hear the *so much more* that He longs to tell you. And it is there God will give you all you need for the *rest* of your life.

After all, there's *no place* like home. Dwelling at home with Him, in your heart.

$\mathcal{R}$emaining in the Secret Place

W E'VE LEARNED THAT REST COMES from a few basic places. Write briefly what you've learned about each element of finding God's peace for your overwhelmed life. Feel free to look at what you've written at the end of the earlier chapters in the book as you write your answers.

Obeying God's command to rest (chapter 1)—

Walking the ancient path (chapter 2)—

Focusing on the few things that matter (chapter 3)—

Surrendering the need to succeed (chapter 4)—

Finding refuge in God's Word (chapter 5)—

Experiencing His peace and power through prayer (chapter 6)—

Refreshing your heart through everyday worship (chapter 7)—

Finding your spacious place (chapter 8)—

Choosing to live a simpler life (chapter 9)—

Standing apart and shining like stars (chapter 10)—

Rediscovering simple pleasures (chapter 11)—

Remaining in your secret place (chapter 12)—

Think of a friend or two who may feel overwhelmed with life right now and need some God-given peace. How can you reach out lovingly toward them in a way that pours rest into their life? (Keep in mind that a talk on what they should do will not go nearly as far as a kind gesture—a note in the mail, some flowers at the door, a kind phone call—letting them know you care and letting them hear God's soothing voice to them, through you.)

Look back through the book and find a favorite verse or two from God's Word that has ministered to you or helped you find rest. Write it here and commit it to memory. (Hiding His Word in your heart is like lovingly decorating your "hideaway" with Him!)

Rest Assured

WE CANNOT TRULY EXPERIENCE REST in our hearts, minds, and lives if we don't have that ultimate question answered in our life: Do I know for sure if I died right now that I would live eternally in God's presence?

God says that when we trust in Jesus Christ's atoning death on the cross and resurrection from the dead, for our salvation, we have entered into His rest. This is the ultimate rest—the rest that comes from the peace and relief of knowing that we will not have to one day pay the penalty for our sin because Jesus already took care of that when He gave His sinless, spotless life in our place. Because of what Jesus did on the cross for *our* sins, when we die, we can live eternally with Him in heaven. That is true rest.

If you are not sure that if you died right now you would live eternally in God's presence, you can pray this prayer, with all your heart, and enter into His rest:

Dear Heavenly Father:

I admit that I am a sinner by nature and there is nothing I can do on my own to make up for that sin in Your holy eyes (Romans 3:23). I accept the sacrifice You provided—

the death of Your righteous and sinless Son, Jesus, on the cross on my behalf, in order to bring me into communion with You. I want to surrender my sin and my life to you and experience Your love and forgiveness toward me. I want to be in a love relationship with You and come to know and love and serve Jesus Christ. I yield to You my right to myself and acknowledge Your right to carry out Your plans for me and to mold me and shape me and transform me for Your pleasure. Thank You for loving me, and please guide me in a new life of loving and obeying You and discovering Your wonderful plan for my life.

I ask these things by faith in the name of Jesus,

Amen.

Welcome to the Resting Place

If you just prayed that prayer to enter into the resting place of a relationship with Jesus Christ, congratulations! The Bible says you are now a part of the family of God, secure in your eternal destiny, beloved of your heavenly Father. Your next step is to grow in that relationship by making sure you fully understand the commitment you made and learning what it means to love, obey, and serve God with all your heart.

Find a pastor or women's ministry director at a Bible-teaching church in your area or a trusted Christian friend and tell him or her of your decision to surrender your life to Christ. They will want to pray for you and give you the support and resources you need to grow in your new relationship with Jesus.

I would love to hear from you as well. Please write or email me your good news. Information about contacting me is on the closing page entitled "An Invitation to Write."

God bless you, my friend, and *rest assured!*

Notes

Chapter One: Following God's Call to Be Still

1. W. E. Vine, *Vine's Expository Dictionary of Old and New Testament Words* (Old Tappan, NJ: Fleming H. Revell Company, 1981), p. 311.

2. See the end of Isaiah 28:12 and Jeremiah 6:16 for examples of when God's people "would not listen" or would "not walk in it."

3. John Eldredge, *Waking the Dead* (Nashville: Thomas Nelson Publishers, 2003), p. 218.

Chapter Two: Finding Soothing Waters on a Slower Path

1. Bill Hybels, *Too Busy Not to Pray* (Downers Grove, IL: InterVarsity Press, 1988), pp. 125-26.

Chapter Three: Focusing on the Few Things That Matter

1. Matthew 6:25-34.

2. Luke 10:41-42 NLT.

3. In John 6:35, Jesus said, "I am the bread of life. He who comes to me will never go hungry, and he who believes in me will never be thirsty."

4. Andrew Stanley, *Choosing to Cheat* (Nashville: Thomas Nelson Publishers, 2002), p. 10.

Chapter Five: Taking Quiet Refuge in God's Word

1. Amy Carmichael, *Whispers of His Power* (Fort Washington, PA: Christian Literature Crusade, 1993), p. 190.

Chapter Six: Experiencing Peace and Power Through Prayer

1. Bill Hybels, *Too Busy Not to Pray* (Downers Grove, IL: InterVarsity Press, 1988), p. 9.

2. Hybels, *Too Busy Not to Pray*, p. 16.

3. Steve Miller, *C.H. Spurgeon on Spiritual Leadership* (Chicago: Moody Publishers, 2003), pp. 26-27.

4. Bill Hybels, *Too Busy Not to Pray*, p. 16.

5. Taken from "What a Friend We Have in Jesus" by Charles C. Converse.

6. Ruth Meyers, *The Perfect Love* (Colorado Springs: WaterBrook Press, 1998), pp. 227-28. Used with permission.

Chapter Seven: Refreshing Your Heart Through Worship

1. Michael W. Smith, *Worship* (Nashville: J. Countryman, 2001), p. 9.
2. First Corinthians 4:7.
3. Matt Redman, *The Unquenchable Worshipper* (Ventura, CA: Gospel Light, 2001), p. 25.
4. Ruth Meyers, *The Perfect Love* (Colorado Springs: WaterBrook Press, 1998), p. 49.

Chapter Eight: Reviving Yourself in a Spacious Place

1. Romans 8:6 THE MESSAGE.
2. Psalm 46:10 NASB.

Chapter Nine: Choosing to Live a Simpler Life

1. A version of this story first appeared in the article "The Right Stuff: What Treasures Are You Collecting?" by Cindi McMenamin in the July/August 1999 issue of *Discipleship Journal*.
2. My husband would prefer that I include "too many shoes" in this list, but for now giving up the Cinderellas was enough! ☺
3. Charles R. Swindoll, *Intimacy with the Almighty* (Nashville: J. Countryman, 1999), p. 27.
4. Swindoll, *Intimacy with the Almighty*, p. 32.
5. For more on doing what God created you to do watch for Cindi's book *When Women Discover their Dream*, available in January 2005 from Harvest House Publishers.

Chapter Ten: Shining like Stars in a Nighttime Sky

1. Lacy McNeil's song "Just Rest" is on her CD, *Provider*, available through her website at www.lacymcneil.com.
2. Jan Meyers, *The Allure of Hope* (Colorado Springs: NavPress, 2001), p. 64.
3. Cindi McMenamin, *When Women Walk Alone* (Eugene, OR: Harvest House Publishers, 2002), pp. 191-92.

Chapter Eleven: Returning to the Joy of Simple Pleasures

1. The Huntington Library and Botanical Gardens is located in San Marino, California.
2. Richard Foster, *Celebration of Discipline* (San Francisco: HarperCollins, 1978), p. 93.

Chapter Twelve: Remaining in the Secret Place

1. Charles R. Swindoll, *Intimacy with the Almighty* (Nashville: J. Countryman, 1999), p. 32.
2. A. W. Tozer, *The Pursuit of God* (Harrisburg, PA: Christian Publications, Inc., 1982), p. 116.

$\mathcal{A}$n Invitation to Write

Cindi McMenamin has a passion for encouraging, inspiring, and motivating women to develop a more intimate relationship with God. If you would like to schedule a one-day conference or "rest retreat" with Cindi, or you would like to share with Cindi how God has used *When Women Long for Rest* in your life, write:

Cindi McMenamin
c/o Harvest House Publishers
990 Owen Loop North
Eugene, Oregon 97402
Email: cindispeaks@msn.com

Other Books by
Cindi McMenamin

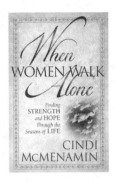

When Women Walk Alone

Every woman—whether she's single or married—has walked through the desert of loneliness. Whether you feel alone from being single, facing challenging life situations, or from being the spiritual head of your household, discover practical steps to finding support, transforming loneliness into spiritual growth, and turning your alone times into life-changing encounters with God.

Letting God Meet Your Emotional Needs

Do you long to have your emotional needs met, yet find that your husband or those close to you cannot always help bring fulfillment to your life? Discover true intimacy with God in this book that shows how to draw closer to the lover of your soul and find that He can, indeed, meet your deepest emotional needs.

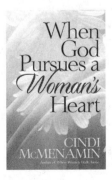

When God Pursues a Woman's Heart

Within the heart of every woman is the desire to be cherished and loved. Recapture the romance of a relationship with God as you discover the many ways God loves you and pursues your heart as your hero, provider, comforter, friend, valiant knight, loving Daddy, perfect prince, and more.